Getting Started with WidgetKit

Create Widgets for iOS and iPadOS

Sagun Raj Lage
Prakshapan Shrestha

Apress®

Getting Started with WidgetKit: Create Widgets for iOS and iPadOS

Sagun Raj Lage
Golmadhi, Bhaktapur, Nepal

Prakshapan Shrestha
Tokha, Kathmandu, Nepal

ISBN-13 (pbk): 978-1-4842-7041-7
https://doi.org/10.1007/978-1-4842-7042-4

ISBN-13 (electronic): 978-1-4842-7042-4

Managing Director, Apress Media LLC: Welmoed Spahr
Acquisitions Editor: Aaron Black
Development Editor: James Markham
Coordinating Editor: Jessica Vakili

Distributed to the book trade worldwide by Springer Science+Business Media New York, 1 NY Plaza, New York, NY 10014. Phone 1-800-SPRINGER, fax (201) 348-4505, e-mail orders-ny@ springer-sbm.com, or visit www.springeronline.com. Apress Media, LLC is a California LLC and the sole member (owner) is Springer Science + Business Media Finance Inc (SSBM Finance Inc). SSBM Finance Inc is a **Delaware** corporation.

For information on translations, please e-mail booktranslations@springernature.com; for reprint, paperback, or audio rights, please e-mail bookpermissions@springernature.com.

Apress titles may be purchased in bulk for academic, corporate, or promotional use. eBook versions and licenses are also available for most titles. For more information, reference our Print and eBook Bulk Sales web page at http://www.apress.com/bulk-sales.

Any source code or other supplementary material referenced by the author in this book is available to readers on GitHub via the book's product page, located at www.apress.com/978-1-4842-7041-7. For more detailed information, please visit http://www.apress.com/source-code.

Printed on acid-free paper

To my father, late Shree Ram Lage, my role model, my inspiration, my pride, who taught me what duties and responsibilities mean. I hope I am making you proud, Baba.

To my mother, Jamuna Laxmi Sitikhu (Lage), my support system, who has befriended struggles and has taught me to bravely face challenges. I know you've made many sacrifices to make me who I am today, Mamu.

To my little sister, Sarina Lage, who has always been there for me in my highs and lows, joys and sorrows. And I know you'll be there for me in the days to come too. I love you.

To my grandparents, Ganga Laxmi Sitikhu and Narayan Bhakta Sitikhu, who have always showered me with their precious blessings and unconditional love.

To my uncles and aunts, Narayan Prasad Sitikhu and Ram Devi Sitikhu, Sunil Kharbuja and Srijana Kharbuja, Krishna Prasad Bohaju and Rejina Bohaju, for wholeheartedly providing their guidance and love to me.

To the person who lit the spark of interest in computers, gadgets, and technology in me since my childhood – my uncle, Jibesh Sitikhu. I wouldn't be where I am today without your contributions, your teachings, your talks and without breaking down your computer many times. And to my aunt, Rajyashwori Sitikhu. You're an epitome of kindness and affection.

To my lovely cousins, Bigyan Sitikhu, Sachin Bohaju, Binam Sitikhu, Salin Bohaju, Shrijal Kharbuja, Jibisha Sitikhu, Swornim Kharbuja, Jibika Sitikhu, Raunak Sitikhu, and Raunika Sitikhu. You have filled my life with joy. I love you all.

To my brother from another mother, Kshitij Raj Lohani, who has always helped me selflessly and who allowed me to access and use his personal MacBook Pro in the United States, from Nepal, for almost a year. I was able to join an iOS bootcamp, write blogs on iOS development, and write this book just because he allowed me to use his computer as I couldn't afford one.

To all my teachers, seniors, mentors, friends, and juniors. You are my gems. I feel blessed to have you in life. Thank you for everything!

—*Sagun Raj Lage*

To my dear mother.

—*Prakshapan Shrestha*

Table of Contents

About the Authors

Sagun Raj Lage started his professional career in software development as a Full Stack Web Developer and later moved into developing iOS applications. He has been a part of development teams on applications used in fields such as transportation, multimedia, shopping, finance, astrology, and management. He is actively involved in organizing developer events and in contributing as a mentor and tutor in programming bootcamps. Apart from software development and programming, he enjoys reading and writing blogs, music, graphic design, and video editing. You can follow him on Twitter at @sagunraj.

Prakshapan Shrestha is an entrepreneurial app developer with 6 years of iOS development experience. He devoutly follows the latest tools and technologies that make a developer's life easier and actively helps out budding developers. Aside from software development, Prakshapan enjoys hiking and spending time with his friends and family. You can follow him on Twitter at @prakshapan.

About the Technical Reviewer

Felipe Laso is a Senior Systems Engineer working at Lextech Global Services. He's also an aspiring game designer/programmer. You can follow him on Twitter at @iFeliLM or on his blog.

Before You Begin...

Before you start exploring the beauty and power of WidgetKit through this book, you will need to make sure you have the following prerequisites set up:

- **A Mac running macOS Catalina (version 10.15.4) or later**: However, we recommend a Mac running macOS Big Sur (version 11) or later as the code was tested on that version.

- **Xcode 12 or later**: Xcode is the primary tool used to develop apps for the Apple ecosystem. You can download the latest version of Xcode from Apple's developer site.[1] We recommend using Xcode 12.4 or later as the code was tested on that version.

- **Swift 5 or later**: Since the new versions of Xcode ship with the updated versions of Swift, you need not worry about this.

- **Simulators and devices with iOS 14 or later installed** since the WidgetKit framework, the framework you will use to develop widgets, is only supported from iOS 14.

---

[1]https://developer.apple.com/xcode/

- **A Twitter Developer Account**: In the last chapter
  of this book, you will develop a widget that will use
  Twitter's API. And you will get access to Twitter's
  API only after you own a Twitter Developer Account.
  You can apply for a developer account from Twitter's
  developer account page.[2]

  Generally, it takes a day or two, or sometimes even
  more, for Twitter to review your application and
  approve or reject it. Therefore, it is a nice idea to
  apply for that account before beginning this book so
  that when you reach the last chapter, your Twitter
  Developer Account will be ready to use.

---

[2]https://developer.twitter.com/en/apply-for-access

CHAPTER 1

Getting Familiar with WidgetKit in a Flash

This chapter will quickly introduce you to WidgetKit, Apple's framework to develop beautiful and handy widgets for iOS homescreen and macOS Notification Center.

Background

WWDC20 brought forward a number of exciting changes and features in the Apple ecosystem. It caught the attention of not only the developers but also of the end users, since it introduced some changes that carry the potential to shape the future of the overall Apple ecosystem experience.

People were anticipating the release of the latest version of iOS in the 20th edition of WWDC, and they got exactly what they were waiting for – iOS 14, a package of awesome features and enhancements! Among those features and enhancements, widgets created a lot of buzz in the market.

Before iOS 14, widgets had very limited features, and they could be seen in a vertical list of full-width boxes on the Today screen (the screen to the left of the first page of the homescreen). That was quite an injustice for

© Sagun Raj Lage and Prakshapan Shrestha 2021
S. R. Lage and P. Shrestha, *Getting Started with WidgetKit*,
https://doi.org/10.1007/978-1-4842-7042-4_1

widgets! But iOS 14 has changed the way iOS treated widgets. Now widgets can contain more information and can show up in various sizes. And the best part is that they are no more confined to be on the Today screen. They can be dragged off the Today screen and placed on the homescreen, together with app icons. And trust us, they look beautiful together.

Now you must be thinking, "Okay, enough of the talks! How can I start?" The next section tells you everything about it.

Hello, WidgetKit!

Apple introduced the WidgetKit framework to enable developers to develop widgets of their apps. The beauty of widgets is that users can get the latest information at a glance, without having to launch the app. And in case users need more details, they can tap on the widget to navigate to the appropriate location in the app.

WidgetKit allows you to create widgets of three different sizes – small, medium, and large. These widgets can be used to display different amount of information. For example, if you have a weather app, you can use the small-sized widget to display only the current temperature in degree Fahrenheit or degree Celsius. The medium-sized widget can display the current location and the temperature. And since the large-sized widget has a greater space, you can use it to display the current location, the temperature, and a brief weather report of the day. And if the users want a detailed report, they can launch the app by tapping the widget. So, for companies, businesses, and developers, widgets are a nice way to keep their users attracted and engaged to their app.

Note   Before developing widgets, you must keep in mind that the WidgetKit framework is available only in iOS 14 and above. So, consider your target users before development. Also, you will require basic SwiftUI knowledge and Xcode 12 or above to be able to develop widgets.

Summary

Now you have gained some familiarity with WidgetKit, Apple's framework to develop widgets of various sizes. Also, you now have an idea about how widgets can help users to get up-to-date information at a glance and how developers can develop beautiful and handy widgets to keep their users attracted and engaged to their app. Plus, you have learned that iOS 14 is the minimum iOS version that supports widgets, and Xcode 12 is the minimum version of Xcode that can be used to develop widgets.

Since SwiftUI is used to develop widgets, in the upcoming chapter, we will give you an overview of SwiftUI and its views that you will use to create widgets. You will learn more about the various sizes of widgets you can create, and you will get an overview of Apple's Human Interface Guidelines (HIG) for widgets.

EXERCISES

1. Go through the overview section of the official documentation of WidgetKit from `https://developer.apple.com/documentation/widgetkit/`. It can help you get a different perspective to understand things. You can explore other sections too, if you are interested.

2. Try completing at least the first chapter, SwiftUI Essentials, from `https://developer.apple.com/tutorials/swiftui/`, if you haven't given SwiftUI a try. This tutorial will help you understand the basics and make you ready for the next chapter of our book.

CHAPTER 2

SwiftUI, Human Interface Guidelines, and Widget Family

Now that you have a general idea about WidgetKit, you can move forward to learn about some basic building blocks of a widget. In this chapter, you will learn about some views of SwiftUI that will act as the building blocks of your widget. Then, you will get an overview of Apple's Human Interface Guidelines for creating intuitive, easy-to-learn, and consistent user interface for widgets. In addition to these, you will learn more about WidgetFamily that enables you to create widgets of various sizes.

SwiftUI

In WWDC 2019, Apple introduced SwiftUI – a framework that brought a major change in the way iOS apps are developed. Before the introduction of SwiftUI, there existed debates between developers about whether they should use Storyboards or develop the app UI programmatically. SwiftUI flushed out the debate and brought a new and easier way to create

S. R. Lage and P. Shrestha, *Getting Started with WidgetKit*,
https://doi.org/10.1007/978-1-4842-7042-4_2

beautiful and interactive user interfaces with eye-pleasing animations and transitions. Note the phrase "new and easier way." There are three major reasons why developing apps using SwiftUI is easier:

1. **SwiftUI uses a declarative approach of programming**: A declarative approach allows you to describe how your app's user interface looks like and what you want your app to do when a state changes, without getting into much details. This decreases the amount of code and makes it easier to read, understand, and modify. Before SwiftUI, we used an imperative approach of programming, meaning that we had to write detailed step-by-step instructions to lay out the user interface and control the states. This generally led to a large volume of code. With SwiftUI, things have become simpler.

2. **Bid farewell to Storyboard and Auto Layout**: Before SwiftUI, developers who didn't prefer developing a user interface programmatically used Storyboard. Using Storyboard was a nice way, but there was a hassle of using Auto Layout to make the app's interface look consistent on all screen sizes. But now, SwiftUI has introduced a number of views (like stacks and spacer) and their properties (like padding) to make user interface appear consistent with lesser effort.

3. **Learn once, apply anywhere**: SwiftUI is a unified user interface framework to build a user interface for all types and sizes of Apple devices. It means that you can easily port the UI code you wrote for

iOS to macOS or watchOS without modifications
or with minimum modifications. Before the launch
of SwiftUI, we had to use different frameworks to
develop apps for different platforms – UIKit for
iOS, AppKit for macOS, WatchKit for watchOS, and
TVUIKit for tvOS.

Due to these reasons, we think that SwiftUI deserves the honor of
being called a lifesaver.

In SwiftUI, views act as the visual building blocks of the user interface
of your app. They are used to display texts, images, shapes, and drawings
in your app. Some views like TextField, Button, Slider, and Picker
even allow users to interact with them to manipulate data and the user
interface. What's more interesting is that you can combine two or more
views to give birth to complex views too.

Widgets are also developed using SwiftUI. So, you will use SwiftUI's
views to bring your widget to life. There is a wide variety of views that you
can use to develop widgets. However, an overview of some basic views that
are used more often will suffice.

Basic SwiftUI Views for Widgets

Let's go through some basic SwiftUI views that are often used to create
widgets.

Text

You can use Text to display one or more lines of read-only text in your app
or widget. For example, if you want your app or widget to display the text
"SwiftUI is fun!", you can write Text("SwiftUI is fun!"). You can also
modify the appearance and size of the text and view by playing with its
methods like font(), italic(), bold(), lineLimit(), and so on.

Button

Button is one of the most commonly used items in user interfaces. It is able to perform an action when it is triggered through events. Its initializer takes two arguments – an action and a label. Let's write some code to create a button that prints "Buttons are good!".

In Listing 2-1, the button contains an action that prints "Buttons are good!" when it is triggered.

Listing 2-1. A button in SwiftUI

```
Button(action: {
     print("Buttons are good!")
}) {
     Text("Tap me")
}
```

The second argument is a Text view that gives the button its title. However, you can use other views here to change the composition of the button and leverage various methods that a button provides to change its appearance and size.

Are you thinking where you can use buttons in your widgets? Assume that you have a to-do list app and your widget needs to display the items that haven't been completed yet. You have planned to represent each item by an empty checkbox, followed by text. So, in this case, you can use a button to create the checkbox, which when tapped removes the item from the to-do list. Simple, right?

Image

The name itself makes it clear that you can use an Image view to display images in your app or widget. In the upcoming lesson, you will create widgets that will display logos of football clubs. And you will use Image views there.

The `Image` view provides various methods to style the image it holds.

You can load an image stored in your Assets.xcassets folder by using the `Image(uiImage: UIImage)` initializer. For example, if the name of the image is "background," you can load it in the `Image` view by writing `Image(uiImage: #imageLiteral(resourceName: "background"))`.

There exists another variety of the `Image` view initializer. It allows you to load system symbol images provided by Apple. The initializer takes a `String` argument, and it is the name of the system symbol image that you want to use.

For example, if you want to load the trash icon, you can use its system symbol name, `"trash"`, and pass it in the initializer by writing `Image(systemName: "trash")`.

Tip   You can use the SF Symbols[1] app to look up the names of system symbol images.

HStack

`HStack` is a view that arranges its child views horizontally. It allows you to create a horizontal stack that arranges the views side by side. In the upcoming chapter, you will use `HStack` to create views that will display the name and the logo of a football club side by side horizontally. In Listing 2-2, you will create an `HStack` that holds a `Text` and a `Button`.

---

[1]https://developer.apple.com/sf-symbols/

Listing 2-2. HStack in action

```
HStack {
    Text("New user?")
    Button(action: {
        print("Register button is tapped.")
    }) {
        Text("Register")
    }
}
```

Listing 2-2 shows an HStack in action. The HStack holds a Text view that displays "New user?", followed by a button displaying "Register." Figure 2-1 shows the screenshot of the result of Listing 2-2.

Figure 2-1. *An HStack displaying a Text and a Button*

In addition, HStack allows you to change the spacing between the items and the alignment of the items.

VStack

VStack enables you to create a vertical stack of views. In the upcoming chapter, you will use VStack to create views that will display the date and time of the upcoming football match in a vertical fashion. The code you will write will be similar to the code given in Listing 2-3.

Listing 2-3. VStack in action

```
VStack {
     Text("On: August 19, 2021")
     Text("At: 6:00 PM")
}
```

Listing 2-3 is the code to create a vertical stack that displays the date and time of the upcoming match. Figure 2-2 shows the screenshot of the result of Listing 2-3.

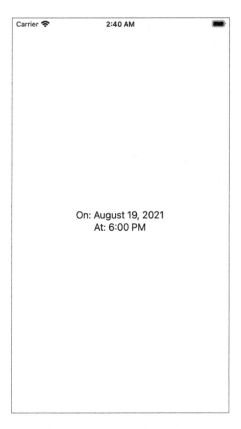

Figure 2-2. *A VStack displaying two Text views*

Like HStack, VStack also allows you to change the spacing between the items and the alignment of the items.

ZStack

Assume that you want to place some text over a picture. That is where ZStack comes into action! ZStack is SwiftUI's special type of stack that overlaps views. Listing 2-4 shows the code to create a ZStack that places the text "Welcome" over a picture.

Listing 2-4. ZStack in action

```
ZStack {
    Image(uiImage: #imageLiteral(resourceName: "welcome-bg"))
    Text("Welcome")
}
```

In Listing 2-4, we have written the Image view before the Text view because we want the Text view to appear over the Image view. Figure 2-3 shows the screenshot of the result of Listing 2-4.

Figure 2-3. *A ZStack displaying a Text view over an Image view*

> **Note**   The view that you want to display on the foreground should be written in the last line of the `ZStack` block.

`ZStack` allows you to change the alignment of the child views that you include in it. However, you cannot change the spacing between the items since it doesn't make sense.

Human Interface Guidelines

Human Interface Guidelines (HIG)[2] are the recommendations Apple gives to the developers for developing apps with intuitive, easy-to-learn, and consistent user interface. You can consider HIG as an instruction manual containing the *dos and don'ts* of user interface development for Apple platforms.

Apple has prepared Human Interface Guidelines for developing widgets too, and they help you understand what the qualities of a good widget are and how you can develop such widgets. In short, the Human Interface Guidelines suggest the following:

- Keep your widget focused upon a specific idea or purpose and use it to display relevant content so that users can get useful information at a glance, without launching the app. Also, avoid creating a widget that simply launches the app, as the app icon already does it. In addition to this, just because WidgetKit allows you to develop various sizes of widgets does not mean that you should always develop widgets of all sizes. Do it only when it adds value to your app.

---

[2]https://developer.apple.com/design/human-interface-guidelines/ios/
system-capabilities/widgets/

- You can allow widgets to be user configurable. But make your widgets configurable only if your widgets require users to configure them so that the widgets can deliver the best output. Another interesting thing about widgets is that you can add tap targets in them to make navigation to relevant screens possible from the widget. However, avoid adding too many tap targets as it may give a bad user experience.

- A widget's main function is to display fresh content. So, make sure to figure out a proper update frequency by analyzing how often changes are seen in the data and by estimating how often people need to see updated data in your widget.

- You can make your widget stand out from the crowd of app icons and widgets by using your brand colors, typefaces, and icons. However, displaying your logo, wordmark, or app icon in the widget does not make sense in most of the cases. Likewise, make sure that the content density does not look crowded and your design elements and colors do not make it difficult for users to see the information your widget is trying to deliver. In addition, adding support for dark mode, giving a realistic preview of the widget along with a proper description, and making use of placeholder content for better user experience create a good impression in front of users.

- Since users using variable-sized devices will install your app and widgets, it is necessary for you to ensure that they adapt well to those screen sizes. For that, size the images you use in your widgets according to the

size table given under the **Size images to look great
on large devices and at high scale factors** heading
in the Human Interface Guidelines for widgets.[3] Also,
ensure that your texts and glyphs adapt well under the
various screen sizes. And use ContainerRelativeShape
to ensure that the content of your widget looks good
within the rounded corners of the widget.

Widget Family

By now, you must have known that the WidgetKit framework allows you
to create widgets of various sizes – small, medium, and large. For this
purpose, you can use a special enum, WidgetFamily. It consists of three
cases – systemSmall, systemMedium, and systemLarge. And by looking at
the names of the cases, you can easily guess which case is responsible for
which size.

This variety in widget sizes gives users the freedom to place and
configure their widgets the way they prefer. Since each widget size can
accommodate different amounts of content and information within it,
it is up to the developers like you to choose what volume of content and
information you would like to display.

Just to give you a bird's eye view at how you can use the three cases of
WidgetFamily to support various widget sizes, we have borrowed some
code from the official documentation[4] and pasted it in Listing 2-5.

---

[3]https://developer.apple.com/design/human-interface-guidelines/ios/
system-capabilities/widgets/

[4]https://developer.apple.com/documentation/widgetkit/staticconfiguration

Listing 2-5. A widget that supports all three widget families

```
struct GameStatusWidget: Widget {
    var body: some WidgetConfiguration {
        StaticConfiguration(
            kind: "com.mygame.game-status",
            provider: GameStatusProvider(),
            placeholder: GameStatusPlaceholderView()
        ) { entry in
            GameStatusView(entry.gameStatus)
        }
        .configurationDisplayName("Game Status")
        .description("Shows an overview of your game status")
        .supportedFamilies([.systemSmall, .systemMedium,
        .systemLarge])
    }
}
```

You can see in Listing 2-5 that a widget named GameStatusWidget has been created. You can ignore other lines and just pay attention to the line that says .supportedFamilies([.systemSmall, .systemMedium, .systemLarge]). This is the line that defines which sizes of widgets your app should support.

supportedFamilies(_:) is an instance method of the WidgetConfiguration protocol. It takes an array of WidgetFamily cases as an argument and is used to set the sizes that a widget supports. Since the StaticConfiguration struct, used in Listing 2-5, conforms to the WidgetConfiguration protocol, it can access supportedFamilies(_:) to set the widget size.

Therefore, in Listing 2-5, the array [.systemSmall, .systemMedium, .systemLarge] has been passed as an argument to supportedFamilies(_:) to set the supported sizes to small, medium, and large.

Tip   We know, you may face difficulties while trying to understand the things we described earlier. But do not worry since we will use them in the exercises of our upcoming chapters. For now, you're doing great!

In case you want your app to support only a single size of widget, that's possible too. Assume that you want your app to support only a medium-sized widget. For that, you can create an array containing a .systemMedium case and pass it to supportedFamilies(_:) by writing .supportedFamilies([.systemMedium]). As simple as that!

Summary

By completing this chapter, you have learned about the SwiftUI views that can be used as building blocks to create widgets of your app. Likewise, you got an overview of Apple's Human Interface Guidelines for widgets that familiarized you with the purpose of widgets and gave you tips to develop intuitive, easy-to-learn, and consistent user interface for widgets. In addition to these, you learned more about WidgetFamily that enables you to create widgets of various sizes.

The next chapter will teach you some important concepts of widgets – timelines and links. But fear not – we are here to guide you!

CHAPTER 3

Writing Your First Widget

Now comes the chapter in which you will finally get to make your hands dirty by working on a project. In this chapter, you will create a widget extension of an existing project and break that widget extension down to see what it is made up of – timeline, timeline provider, widget view, placeholder, snapshot, and widget configuration.

We have prepared a starter project so that you can get straight into creating its widget. Find the zip file named **SoccerTime.zip** and unzip it to get started with the project.

If you've successfully unzipped **SoccerTime.zip** and opened the **SoccerTime.xcodeproj** file of the **SoccerTimeStarter** folder, you will know that **SoccerTime** is the project we will be working on. **SoccerTime** is an app that displays the details of the upcoming soccer matches of your favorite teams. It consists of two screens – one for adding upcoming matches (Figure 3-1) and the other for displaying a list of the matches you add (Figure 3-2). Launch the app and add some matches with future date to understand the features more clearly.

© Sagun Raj Lage and Prakshapan Shrestha 2021
S. R. Lage and P. Shrestha, *Getting Started with WidgetKit*,
https://doi.org/10.1007/978-1-4842-7042-4_3

Figure 3-1. *The screen that displays the list of upcoming matches in SoccerTime*

Figure 3-2. *The screen from where users add their favorite upcoming matches*

Now here comes the interesting part – you will create **SoccerTime**'s widget that will display information about the forthcoming matches you add in the app. You will create a small-sized widget that will display the logos of the two teams competing in the nearest upcoming match and a countdown before the match begins. The widget will look like Figure 3-3.

Figure 3-3. *The small-sized widget of SoccerTime*

So, the first step is to add a widget extension to the project, and the upcoming section describes everything about it.

Widget Extension

The widget extension is a template that provides a basic structure and boilerplate code to help you get started with creating your app's widget. It holds the widgets that you create. Apple recommends developers to include all the widgets of an app in a single widget extension. However, it's also possible to create multiple widget extensions, if necessary.

To create a widget extension of SoccerTime, follow the steps given as follows:

1. Open **SoccerTime.xcodeproj**.

2. Go to **File ➤ New ➤ Target ➤ iOS**.

3. You can either scroll down or use filter to find **Widget Extension**. Then double-click it.

4. Now a dialog box will appear where you will do the following:

   a. Set **Product Name** to **SoccerTimeWidget**.

   b. Set **Team** to either **None** or choose your team.

   c. Uncheck **Include Configuration Intent**.

   d. Make sure that **SoccerTime** is the selected **Project**.

   e. Verify that **SoccerTime** is the selected application in the **Embed in Application** field.

   f. Click **Finish**.

5. Once you click finish, the widget extension gets generated, and Xcode will ask one final question, "Activate 'SoccerTimeWidgetExtension' scheme?". Click **Agree** so that that scheme is activated. The change you will see in your Xcode screen after that is shown in Figure 3-4.

Figure 3-4. *A screenshot displaying SoccerTimeWidgetExtension as the selected scheme*

After you've followed the steps mentioned earlier, the first thing you will notice is the addition of the **SoccerTimeWidget** folder in the project. This is where everything related to your widgets is kept.

From the **SoccerTimeWidget** folder, open **SoccerTimeWidget.swift** to see the boilerplate code of the building blocks of your widget. You will be making changes in this file to customize your widget. Now, we will give you an overview of all the blocks in **SoccerTimeWidget.swift**. Also, we will guide you to make changes in that file so that you can create widgets that will allow users to see the details of the upcoming matches in their homescreen.

Note   Notice in the Target Membership section of File Inspector that **SoccerTimeWidget.swift** has its target set to **SoccerTimeWidgetExtension** instead of the **SoccerTime**.

TimelineEntry

`TimelineEntry` is a protocol that specifies when a widget should be displayed. It consists of a `date` property for indicating that. Also, it can help the system determine the relevance of the widget's content. These capabilities of `TimelineEntry` are capitalized by `TimelineProvider` by managing one or more timeline entries to tell WidgetKit when to display a widget. Then, WidgetKit renders the widget by executing the `content` block of the widget configuration, passing the corresponding timeline entry.

Note   We know that you aren't familiar with `TimelineProvider` and `WidgetConfiguration` yet, but you will get to know them in the upcoming sections. For now, you can just keep in mind that `TimelineProvider` manages timeline entries and `WidgetConfiguration` is the place from where you configure the widget.

To use the features of `TimelineEntry`, you create a struct that conforms to it. Since it is a type of model that `WidgetConfiguration` will require to render the widget, you have to make sure you add all the properties that `WidgetConfiguration` will need.

In the current project, if you go to **SoccerTime ➤ Model ➤ Match. swift**, you will see a model that the app is using to store details about a match. Since your widget will display the same details that Match helps to store, you can use this model.

If you look at the structure of Match, you will notice that it conforms to Codable and Identifiable protocols. Now, to make it usable even as a timeline entry, make it conform to the TimelineEntry protocol. For that, WidgetKit needs to be imported first. So, in **Match.swift**, add the line import WidgetKit at the first line.

Then, make Match conform to TimelineEntry by modifying it and making it look like Listing 3-1.

Listing 3-1. Making a model conform to TimelineEntry

```
struct Match: Codable, Identifiable, TimelineEntry {
     var id = UUID()
     var primaryClub: String
     var secondaryClub: String
     var date: Date
}
```

If you build the project right now, you will encounter an error saying, "Match does not conform to protocol 'TimelineEntry.'" It is because a struct conforming to TimelineEntry compulsorily needs to have a date property of Date type. If you look thoroughly at Match, you will see that there already is a property of Date type, that is, time. So, you can rename it to date since the time property was there for the same purpose – to store date.

Now build the project and you will see that the renaming affected the whole project. You will see errors in ListMatchView, MatchCell, and AddMatchView. Rename time to date in all those places and build the project to find all errors gone.

TimelineProvider

TimelineProvider can be considered as the driving force of the widget. It is a protocol that lets WidgetKit know when it should update a widget's display. It fetches entries of type TimelineEntry and displays each entry at the time stored in the entry's date property.

Now, you will create a struct that conforms to TimelineProvider. But before that, create a folder named **SmallWidget** in the **SoccerTimeWidget** folder to store all the files related to the small variant of your widget.

Then, in the **SmallWidget** folder, create a Swift file and name it **SmallWidgetDataProvider**. Before clicking Create, make sure to check **SoccerTimeWidgetExtension** in the Targets section so that **SmallWidgetDataProvider** becomes available in your widget extension too.

Now, open **SmallWidgetDataProvider.swift** and replace the existing code from that file with the code in Listing 3-2.

Listing 3-2. Creating SmallWidgetDataProvider

```
import SwiftUI
import WidgetKit

struct SmallWidgetDataProvider: TimelineProvider {

}
```

Listing 3-2 imports SwiftUI and WidgetKit and creates a struct named SmallWidgetDataProvider that conforms to TimelineProvider.

Now, you'll see an error saying "Type 'SmallWidgetDataProvider' does not conform to protocol 'TimelineProvider'." It is because you still haven't implemented the methods of that protocol. For now, you can ignore that error.

Now add the line typealias Entry = Match to
SmallWidgetDataProvider. That line implements the Entry typealias
property of the TimelineProvider protocol in SmallWidgetDataProvider.
As stated earlier, this is how you are feeding SmallWidgetDataProvider (a
timeline provider) a timeline entry (Match). Build the project.

Now you must be seeing a new error that says, "Cannot find type
'Match' in scope." The reason behind this error is that **Match.swift** is not
a member of the **SoccerTimeWidgetExtension** target, hence not being
available in your widget extension. If you open **Match.swift**, you will see
in the Target Membership section of File Inspector that only **SoccerTime**
has been checked, and not **SoccerTimeWidgetExtension**. Right now, the
Target Membership section looks like Figure 3-5.

Figure 3-5. *A screenshot displaying Match.swift's target membership*

Since you need to use `Match` in **SoccerTimeWidgetExtension** too, add a checkmark on it.

It's time to get rid of the only remaining error saying, "Type 'SmallWidgetDataProvider' does not conform to protocol 'TimelineProvider'." Open the error and click **Fix**. Then it will generate the boilerplate code of `TimelineProvider`'s methods, and the code will look similar to Listing 3-3.

Listing 3-3. Boilerplate code of SmallWidgetDataProvider

```
import WidgetKit
import SwiftUI

struct SmallWidgetDataProvider: TimelineProvider {

    typealias Entry = Match

    func placeholder(in context: Context) -> Match {
        <#code#>
    }

    func getSnapshot(in context: Context, completion: @escaping
    (Match) -> Void) {
        <#code#>
    }

    func getTimeline(in context: Context, completion: @escaping
    (Timeline<Match>) -> Void) {
        <#code#>
    }

}
```

Listing 3-3 shows the code of SmallWidgetDataProvider. There is boilerplate code of the three methods of TimelineProvider (that SmallWidgetDataProvider conforms to), and it's the developer's job to write their implementations. The basic overview of those methods is given as follows, along with some hands-on work for you.

placeholder(in:)

A placeholder displays a generic representation of your widget view during its first load after being added to the homescreen. It can also be displayed while your widget is in the process of retrieving new data.

In WidgetKit, the placeholder(in:) method of TimelineProvider is responsible to return a placeholder timeline entry.

Let's give it a try. After the line that says typealias Entry = Match in SmallWidgetDataProvider, create a variable placeholderEntry of Match type that returns a placeholder timeline entry. It is shown in Listing 3-4.

Listing 3-4. Declaration of a placeholderEntry variable

```
var placeholderEntry: Match {
    return Match(primaryClub: "none",
                 secondaryClub: "none",
                 date: Date())
}
```

As stated earlier, Listing 3-4 declares a variable placeholderEntry of Match type and returns a Match object (that conforms to TimelineEntry) with primaryClub and secondaryClub values set to "none" and the current date.

Note   It's not compulsory to create a `placeholderEntry` variable, but since you will be using this same object in multiple places, it's a nice idea to create and store the object in a variable.

Now you can update the `placeholder(in:)` method to make it appear like Listing 3-5.

Listing 3-5. placeholder(in:) method

```
func placeholder(in context: Context) -> Match {
    return placeholderEntry
}
```

In Listing 3-5, the `placeholder(in:)` method has been modified to make it return the `placeholderEntry` variable you had declared in Listing 3-4.

getSnapshot(in:completion:)

iOS 14 comes with a widget gallery that displays the previews of the widgets of all the apps in a device. From there, users can choose the widget they want to show in their homescreen. For a widget, the widget gallery is the platform to display its realistic preview and flaunt its beauty and capabilities so that users can come to an informed decision about whether to add it to their homescreen or not.

The `getSnapshot(in:completion:)` method of `TimelineProvider` is what provides widgets the facility of flaunting their preview in the widget gallery, when `context.isPreview` is set to `true`. This method is called whenever the widget is in a transient state like appearing in the widget gallery or waiting for data. So, it's necessary to make sure that this method doesn't contain heavy calculations.

In addition to this, getSnapshot(in:completion:) provides a timeline entry representing the current time and state of a widget. So, using this method, you will fetch the latest upcoming match to be displayed in your widget. For that, you will have to fetch the current state of the widget using a new method and perform calculation to get the latest upcoming match. So, in SmallWidgetDataProvider, define the getLatestUpcomingMatch() method right below the placeholder variable and write the code in Listing 3-6.

Listing 3-6. Definition of the getLatestUpcomingMatch() method

```swift
func getLatestUpcomingMatch() -> Match {
    if let matches: [Match] = AppUtils.
    fetchDataWith(fileName: "Matches.json") {

        let upcomingMatches = matches.filter({ $0.date >
        Date() })

        let sortedMatches = upcomingMatches.sorted(by: {
        $0.date < $1.date })

        if let firstUpcomingMatch = sortedMatches.first {

            return firstUpcomingMatch
        }
    }

    return placeholderEntry
}
```

Listing 3-6 defines the getLatestUpcomingMatch() method, and the following operations take place in it:

1. When you save matches in the app, all of those data are stored in JSON format in a file called **Matches.json**. So, in this step, you are checking if that file exists or not using the fetchDataWith(filename:) method of AppUtils. One thing to note is that the JSON file could be stored in the document directory of the app. But since more than one target (**SoccerTime** and **SoccerTimeWidget**) needs to access that file, it had to be stored in a container. Hence, to access the file in the container, the getSharedDocumentsDirectory() method was created in AppUtils, and it has been called by fetchDataWith(filename:). So, if the JSON file exists, then you move forward; else placeholderEntry is returned.

Note   As you will be using AppUtils in your widget extension, make sure to update its **Target Membership** to **SoccerTimeWidgetExtension** as well.

---

2. In step 2, you're filtering the matches with future dates.

3. Now matches are sorted in ascending order on the basis of time. Hence, the match with the date nearest to the current date lies at the first index, and the match with the farthest date stays at last.

4. Finally, the first match from the sorted array of matches is fetched and returned.

Now, update the getSnapshot(in:completion:) method as shown in Listing 3-7 to give it the finishing touch.

Listing 3-7. Modification of the getSnapshot(in:completion:) method

```
func getSnapshot(in context: Context, completion: @escaping
(Match) -> Void) {
    completion(getLatestUpcomingMatch())
}
```

Listing 3-7 modifies the getSnapshot(in:completion:) method to make it return the nearest upcoming match and, hence, display it in the widget preview shown in the widget gallery. If no upcoming matches have been added in the app, the widget preview displays, "No upcoming matches."

getTimeline(in:completion:)

getTimeline(in:completion:) is the brain of TimelineProvider. It provides an array of timeline entries for the current time and, optionally, any future times to update a widget. Moreover, it sets the timeline reload policy of the widget to user preferred time. The reload policy determines when to update the timeline to refresh the content being displayed in your widget. There are three reload policies that are available:

1. never: This policy updates the widget when a new timeline is available.

2. atEnd: It requests a new timeline after the date specified in the last timeline passes.

3. after: This policy requests a new timeline at a specified date.

The never refresh policy can be used in cases when you cannot predict the date for refreshing the widget content. In that situation, WidgetKit doesn't request a new timeline, and when a new timeline becomes available at some point, it calls reloadTimelines(of Kind:) of the WidgetCenter class. For example, it makes sense to use never when a widget's content is dependent on the user being logged in to an account, but they aren't logged in.

But the case is different with atEnd and after. They are used when future events are predictable and you know when to update the widget's content. To explain this, the official documentation gives an example of a widget displaying stock market details.[1] It says that it is a nice idea to use atEnd or after in such a scenario because you can specify the next date when the stock market opens or closes since the information generally does not change overnight or during weekends.

Enough of the explanation. Now, modify the getTimeline(in:completion:) method as shown in Listing 3-8.

Listing 3-8. Modification of the getTimeline(in:completion:) method

```
func getTimeline(in context: Context, completion: @escaping
(Timeline<Match>) -> Void) {
    // 1
    let entry = getLatestUpcomingMatch()
    // 2
    let refresh = Calendar.current.date(byAdding: .second,
    value: 1, to: entry.date)
```

----

[1]https://developer.apple.com/documentation/widgetkit/timelineprovider

```
// 3
let timeline = Timeline(entries: [entry],
policy: .after(refresh!))
// 4
completion(timeline)
}
```

In the code of Listing 3-8, the following tasks are being done:

1. The nearest upcoming match is fetched using
   getLatestUpcomingMatch(), and the fetched value
   is stored in entry.

2. Then, the next refresh time is set to be a second later
   than entry's date.

3. In the third step, a timeline is created with entry
   and an after refresh policy. The refresh policy is set
   to be after the time we set up in step 2.

4. Finally, the timeline is handed over to the widget.

In this way, the configuration of SmallWidgetDataProvider, a class
conforming to TimelineProvider, is complete. Now, it's time to develop
the user interface of the widget using SwiftUI.

Developing Your Widget's UI

The last sections were all about configuring the working mechanism of
your widget. In this section, you will finally work on the user interface of
your widget. You will be making a small-sized widget, and the view you will
be creating is basically the same as the one normally made with SwiftUI,
but with some small tweaks. The widget will display the logos of the two
teams competing in the nearest upcoming match and a countdown before
the match begins.

Start by creating a SwiftUI file. Navigate to the **SmallWidget** folder and then create a **SwiftUI View** named **SmallWidgetView** by going to **File ➤ New ➤ File… ➤ SwiftUI View**. After setting the filename and choosing the location, before clicking **Create**, remember to put a checkmark on the **SoccerTimeWidgetExtension** target at the bottom of the dialog box.

After **SmallWidgetView.swift** is created, replace its content by the code given in Listing 3-9.

Listing 3-9. SmallWidgetView.swift

```
// 1
import SwiftUI
import WidgetKit

struct SmallWidgetView: View {
    // 2
    var match: SmallWidgetDataProvider.Entry
    var body: some View {
        // 3
        VStack(alignment: .center) {
        HStack() {
            Club(value: match.primaryClub)
.logo.resizable()
.aspectRatio(contentMode: .fit)
            Text("vs").font(.footnote)
            Club(value: match.secondaryClub)
.logo.resizable()
.aspectRatio(contentMode: .fit)
        }.frame(height: 50)
        if match.date > Date() {
            Text(match.date, style: .timer)
                .font(.system(.title,
```

```
design: .monospaced))
                        .foregroundColor(Color.gray)
                    .multilineTextAlignment(.center)
            } else {
                Text("No upcoming matches.")
.foregroundColor(.gray)
            }
        }
    }
}
```

Listing 3-9 is the code that lays out the user interface of your small-sized widget. However, you must have seen an error saying "Cannot find 'Club' in scope" after pasting the code. To fix this, you need to make Club available in the SoccerTimeWidgetExtension target, and by now you must have had at least some blurry idea about how to do it. But it's okay if you haven't been able to figure it out yet. Just go to the **Clubs.swift** file and put checkmarks on both **SoccerTime** and **SoccerTimeWidgetExtension** in the Target Membership of File Inspector. Also, do the same and update the target membership of **Assets.xcassets** (located in the **SoccerTime** folder) and **ImageExtension.swift** (located in the **Extension** folder) by checking **SoccerTimeWidgetExtension** to avoid the errors like "Type 'Image' has no member 'alavés'."

Now, let us explain what the code in Listing 3-9 does:

1. Imports SwiftUI and WidgetKit.

2. Declares a variable named match, which will be used to provide data to the view. In the current case, the data are TimelineEntry values from SmallWidgetDataProvider.

3. The view is prepared using VStack and HStack to show the information provided by the match. If the entry's date is not greater than the current time, then "No upcoming matches." is shown instead of a timer.

Till now, the **Canvas** window of **SmallWidgetView** must be saying "No Preview." It is because you removed the preview struct of SmallWidgetView while replacing its content with the code of Listing 3-9. Now, fix it by pasting the code in Listing 3-10 at the bottom of the file.

Listing 3-10. Preview struct of SmallWidgetView

```
struct SmallWidgetView_Previews: PreviewProvider {
    static var previews: some View {
        SmallWidgetView(match: Match(primaryClub: "",
        secondaryClub: "", date: Date()))
      .previewContext(WidgetPreviewContext(family:
      .systemSmall))
    }
}
```

The code in Listing 3-10 creates a preview of SmallWidgetView, and as soon as you paste it and click **Resume** in the **Canvas** window, a preview like the one shown in Figure 3-6 is displayed.

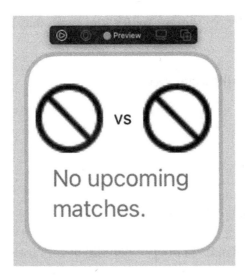

Figure 3-6. *A screenshot displaying the preview of small-sized widget*

WidgetConfiguration

Now it's time to put everything together and make the widget work. For that, you will need to add an entry point, that is, a struct conforming to the Widget protocol and marked by the @main property wrapper. This struct will contain a body with an instance of WidgetConfiguration, and that is where you will join all the pieces together and configure your widget.

To create this entry point, navigate to the **SmallWidget** folder and create a **SwiftUI View** named **SmallWidget** and also make sure you add a checkmark to **SoccerTimeWidgetExtension** in Targets before creating that file. Also, in Targets, if **SoccerTime** is checked, uncheck it.

Tip   If you face confusions while creating a SwiftUI View, refer to the second paragraph of "Developing Your Widget's UI" section.

Now, replace the content of **SmallWidget** with the code given in Listing 3-11.

Listing 3-11. SmallWidget.swift

```swift
import WidgetKit
import SwiftUI

// 1
@main
struct SmallWidget: Widget {
    // 2
    let widgetKind: String = "SmallSoccerTimeWidget"

    // 3
    var body: some WidgetConfiguration {
      StaticConfiguration(kind: widgetKind,
       provider: SmallWidgetDataProvider()) { match
            in
    // 4
          SmallWidgetView(match: match)
      }
    // 5
      .configurationDisplayName("Mini Widget")
      .description("Shows upcoming match.")
      .supportedFamilies([.systemSmall])
    }
}
```

In Listing 3-11, the following things are done:

1. SwiftUI and WidgetKit are imported, and a struct SmallWidget conforming to Widget is created. Then, SmallWidget is marked using the @main property wrapper to let the system know that it is the entry point for the target. In other words, the code execution for rendering the small widget starts from here.

2. widgetKind is defined using a unique string. It is used to describe your widget.

3. A Widget's body should be an instance of WidgetConfiguration. Since both StaticConfiguration and IntentConfiguration (to be discussed later) conform to WidgetConfiguration, any of them can be used. For now, you have used StaticConfiguration, providing it widgetKind as kind and SmallWidgetDataProvider as provider.

4. In this step, it's been written that SmallWidgetView will act as the view of the widget, and it has been provided with a timeline entry, match.

5. In the fifth step, a configuration display name and a description have been provided to the widget, and they are displayed above your widget when users see it in the widget gallery. The preview of how the widget looks in the widget gallery is shown in Figure 3-7. Also, since the goal is to just support the small-sized widget, an array containing only the systemSmall variety of WidgetFamily is passed to the supportedFamilies() method.

Figure 3-7. *The preview of a small-sized widget of SoccerTime in the widget gallery*

This completes the setup of the widget. Now build and run to see the results of your effort.

Note   Before running, make sure that the currently selected scheme is **SoccerTimeWidgetExtension**. For reference, refer to Figure 3-4. If **SoccerTime** is the selected scheme, the app will run, not the widget.

But it doesn't run, does it? This is because there are two entry points for your widget right now. Delete the boilerplate file **SoccerTimeWidget. swift**, created by Xcode when you had first generated the widget extension. Now build and run again.

Now it should run and your simulator should display the small-sized widget in its homescreen, and it should look similar to Figure 3-8.

Figure 3-8. *A screenshot of the small-sized widget in the homescreen*

You can play around with the widget and the application. Currently, you may see bugs and limitations, but we will address them one after another in the upcoming chapters.

Summary

Congratulations on making it this far! This might have been a challenging chapter for you, but no matter how hard it was, you made it. By completing this chapter, you have created your very first widget for iOS using SwiftUI. Also, you have gained some familiarity with the building blocks of widgets like timeline, timeline provider, widget view, placeholder, snapshot, and widget configuration. To sum up, a widget is made up of three core components:

1. **Views**: SwiftUI views that are used by WidgetKit as a user interface

2. **TimelineProvider**: A protocol responsible to update the widget content according to the context passed at a specified date

3. **WidgetConfiguration**: Binds all the building blocks of a widget together and configures the widget

You may still have confusions about things, but have patience and practice more. And please refer to the final code of the project in the **SoccerTimeFinal** folder of the **SoccerTime.zip** file. Plus, you don't have to worry as you will use those concepts in the upcoming chapters as well.

The next chapter will teach you about links which will enable users to tap on your widget and navigate to a relevant screen in your app for getting more details about the content shown in your widget. Till then, keep up the good work!

CHAPTER 4

Making Widgets Configurable and Interactive

One special thing about widgets is that users can configure them and also interact with them to some extent. In this chapter, you will learn how you can make your widget configurable and interactive so that users will fall in love with your widget. To make your widget configurable, you will use IntentConfiguration. And you will make the views in your widget tappable so that users can tap them and navigate to various screens using deep links. As this chapter has a lot of important things to cover, you may find it longer than other chapters of this book. So, it is a good idea to give this chapter some days and even perform revisions.

Let's Get Started

To begin working, you can unzip the file named **OnThisDay.zip**. If you've successfully unzipped it, open the **OnThisDayStarter** folder and run **OnThisDay.xcodeproj** to see **OnThisDay** in action. OnThisDay is an application that displays the events that historically took place on the

© Sagun Raj Lage and Prakshapan Shrestha 2021
S. R. Lage and P. Shrestha, *Getting Started with WidgetKit*,
https://doi.org/10.1007/978-1-4842-7042-4_4

system date, by making use of Wikipedia's "On This Day REST API."[1] It lists various types of events like births, deaths, events, holidays, and selected events under their respective section headers. Figures 4-1 and 4-2 give you an idea of how the app actually looks.

Figure 4-1. *The homescreen of OnThisDay displaying a list of birthdays*

---

[1]https://en.wikipedia.org/api/rest_v1/#/Feed/onThisDay

Figure 4-2. *The homescreen of OnThisDay displaying a list of section headers*

Another interesting feature of **OnThisDay** is that you can choose the type of the event and get a filtered list of the events of that particular type. And that choice stays persistent even after you close and rerun the app – meaning that if you choose **Selected** from the menu, even when you close and rerun the app, only **Selected** events will be displayed in the list. Thanks to UserDefaults[2] for making this possible! Figure 4-3 displays a menu from which you can select a type or category of events.

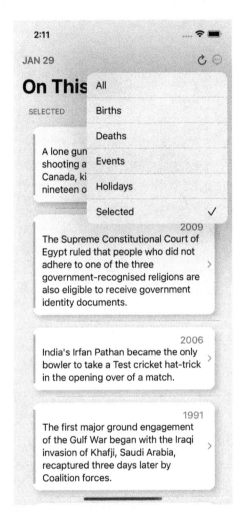

Figure 4-3. *Choosing "Selected" events from the menu*

---

[2]https://developer.apple.com/documentation/foundation/userdefaults

Also, you can tap on an event to see more details and a photo related to that event. Refer to Figure 4-4 to see the screenshot of the event detail screen. **OnThisDay** also shows the pages related to that event, and you can tap on those pages to navigate to their Wikipedia pages. That screen is shown in Figure 4-5.

Figure 4-4. *A detail screen displayed after tapping an event on the homescreen*

Figure 4-5. *A Wikipedia page loaded after tapping a "Related Page" in the detail screen*

Now you must have deduced that **OnThisDay** is a fully functional app. Yes, it is. But, why not create its widgets and display some information on the user's homescreen? Widgets surely can help to make your app look more useful to the user. That is why we have done some part of the work for you. We have already created a widget extension of OnThisDay as **OnThisDayWidgetExtension** and written all three families of widgets for **OnThisDay**. Choose the **OnThisDayWidgetExtension** scheme and run the code to see the small widget of OnThisDay on your simulator's or device's homescreen (Figure 4-6).

Figure 4-6. *A screenshot displaying OnThisDayWidgetExtension as the selected scheme*

Add the other two widget families also to your homescreen by long pressing a space in the homescreen and tapping the "+" icon. Then from the app list, tap OnThisDay and scroll to your desired widget family and tap **Add Widget**.

Currently, the widgets are displaying dummy data, but later you will integrate Wikipedia's "On This Day REST API" to display updated information.

Now, let's move on to how the widgets look like. The small widget (Figure 4-7), as it has less space, displays only the number of events that took place historically on the system date.

Figure 4-7. *Small-sized widget of OnThisDay*

But since the medium widget (Figure 4-8) can accommodate some more views, it not only shows the number of events that took place historically on the system date but also some information about a couple of events.

***Figure 4-8.** Medium-sized widget of OnThisDay*

And the large widget (Figure 4-9) displays the same information that the medium widget displays, but in a greater amount and a different arrangement.

***Figure 4-9.** Large-sized widget of OnThisDay*

In addition to this, at the later part of this chapter, you will make your widgets configurable – meaning that users will be able to long press on your widgets and **Edit Widget** to select the type/category of events whose information they would like the widget to display. Hence, if the users select **Holidays**, only the information of the events lying in the "Holidays" category will be displayed in the widget. Figure 4-10 is the screenshot of the widget displaying the list of options given when a widget is long pressed, and Figure 4-11 is the screenshot of the widget displaying the configuration option shown after tapping **Edit Widget**. In addition to these, Figure 4-12 shows the event categories that users can choose from to make their widget display information about.

Figure 4-10. *The list of options displayed when a widget is long pressed*

Figure 4-11. *The configuration option displayed after tapping Edit Widget in Figure 4-10*

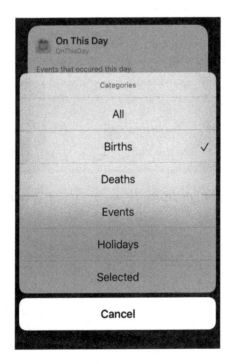

Figure 4-12. *The event categories users can choose from to make the widget display information about*

Now, it's time that you look at the already existing code. As we have already stated earlier, we have already set up some basic stuff.

If you go to the **Project Navigator** and open the **OnThisDay** project, you will find two main folders, that is, **OnThisDay** and **OnThisDayWidget**. The **OnThisDay** folder contains the files and folders related to the app, and the **OnThisDayWidget** folder contains the files and folders related to the widgets. There are also certain files which are used by both the app and the widgets, and those files are shared using **Target Membership**.

Open the **OnThisDay** folder in the **OnThisDay** project to see the following folder structure:

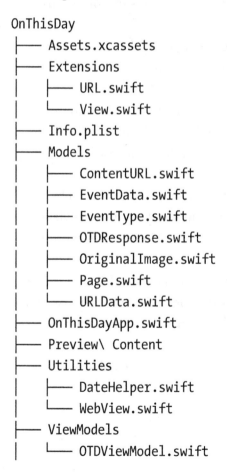

```
OnThisDay
├── Assets.xcassets
├── Extensions
│   ├── URL.swift
│   └── View.swift
├── Info.plist
├── Models
│   ├── ContentURL.swift
│   ├── EventData.swift
│   ├── EventType.swift
│   ├── OTDResponse.swift
│   ├── OriginalImage.swift
│   ├── Page.swift
│   └── URLData.swift
├── OnThisDayApp.swift
├── Preview\ Content
├── Utilities
│   ├── DateHelper.swift
│   └── WebView.swift
├── ViewModels
│   └── OTDViewModel.swift
```

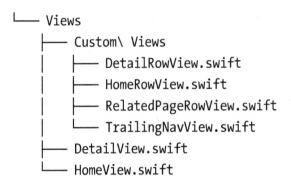

```
└── Views
    ├── Custom\ Views
    │   ├── DetailRowView.swift
    │   ├── HomeRowView.swift
    │   ├── RelatedPageRowView.swift
    │   └── TrailingNavView.swift
    ├── DetailView.swift
    └── HomeView.swift
```

You will see **Assets.xcassets** and **Info.plist** in that folder. Likewise, there is a folder called **Extensions** that stores the extensions of various structs.

In addition to these, there is a **Models** folder that contains the files used to parse the response data received after calling Wikipedia's API endpoint.

OnThisDayApp.swift is the main entry point of your app, and the **Preview Content** folder is a folder generated by Xcode to store the assets used for development purposes. The files in this folder are not included by Xcode in release builds.

There is a **Utilities** folder, and it contains various utilities used by the app for serving purposes like working with dates and loading webview.

And the **ViewModel** folder contains **OTDViewModel.swift**, the view model for the app.

Finally, the **Views** folder contains a number of files and folders. There are various small views stored in the **Custom Views** folder, and those views are used by **HomeView.swift** and **DetailView.swift**, which contain the user interface of the app.

That's the description of the folder and files in the **OnThisDay** folder.

Now, open the **OnThisDayWidget** folder to see the following folder structure:

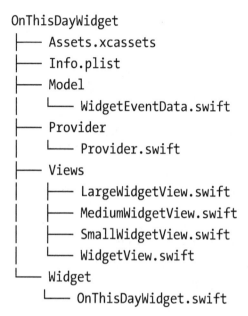

```
OnThisDayWidget
├── Assets.xcassets
├── Info.plist
├── Model
│   └── WidgetEventData.swift
├── Provider
│   └── Provider.swift
├── Views
│   ├── LargeWidgetView.swift
│   ├── MediumWidgetView.swift
│   ├── SmallWidgetView.swift
│   └── WidgetView.swift
└── Widget
    └── OnThisDayWidget.swift
```

Other than the **Assets.xcassets** folder and **Info.plist** file, you will see a folder called **Model** that contains **WidgetEventData.swift**. This model contains a TimelineEntry called WidgetEvent which is vital for your widgets to work.

Likewise, there is a folder called **Provider** containing **Provider.swift**, which is the TimelineProvider of the widgets. If you remember, it is what drives a widget by fetching TimelineEntry values.

The next folder that you can see is **Views**, and it contains **LargeWidgetView.swift**, **MediumWidgetView.swift**, **SmallWidgetView. swift**, and **WidgetView.swift**. Those files contain the user interface of your widgets. The **WidgetView.swift** file is the main file that determines which view should be rendered when a particular widget family is chosen by users.

And lastly, the Widget folder contains the **OnThisDayWidget.swift** file, which is the entry point for the **OnThisDayWidgetExtension** target. It is currently using StaticConfiguration, which you will replace with IntentConfiguration to make your widgets configurable.

Giving Widgets the Power to Talk to API

In this section, you will remove dummy data from your widgets and give them the capability to call Wikipedia's "On This Day API" to fetch fresh data and to display latest information. For now, do not worry about the categories/types of events as you will make your widget fetch and display information about all types of events.

1. Create a new file named **OnThisDayAPI.swift** in the **Provider** folder of **OnThisDayWidget**. Make sure that the **OnThisDayWidgetExtension** target is checked along with the **OnThisDay** target while creating this file.

2. Copy and paste the code in Listing 4-1 to that file to create an OnThisDayAPI struct with a static fetchOnThisDayData(with:) method.

Listing 4-1. OnThisDayAPI struct with a static method to call Wikipedia's API

```
struct OnThisDayAPI {
    static func fetchOnThisDayData(with completion: @escaping
    ([WidgetEventData]) -> Void) {
        guard let today = DateHelper.getDayAndMonthInNumbers(),
            let url = URL(string: "https://en.wikipedia.org/
            api/rest_v1/feed/onthisday/all/\(today.month)/
            \(today.day)") else { return }
```

```swift
    let task = URLSession.shared.dataTask(with: url) {
data, response, _ in
        if let data = data,
            let response = response as? HTTPURLResponse,
            response.statusCode == 200 {
            do {
                let otdResponse = try JSONDecoder().
                decode(OTDResponse.self, from: data)
                var responses: [EventData] = []
                responses = otdResponse.selected +
                otdResponse.births + otdResponse.deaths +
                otdResponse.events + otdResponse.holidays
                completion(responses.map({ WidgetEventData
                (text: $0.text) }))
            } catch {
                completion([])
                print("JSON Decoding Error.")
            }
            completion([])
        }
    }
    task.resume()
  }
}
```

Listing 4-1 consists of the OnThisDayAPI struct that contains a static method named fetchOnThisDayData(with:). This method calls Wikipedia's API to fetch all types of events that took place on the system date that is returned by the DateHelper.getDayAndMonthInNumbers() method and stored in the today variable. Then the response is decoded, and it is returned to the caller using its completion handler that takes an array of WidgetEventData as an argument.

Now, since you have fetchOnThisDayData(with:) ready, it's time to call it. Go to **Provider.swift** and replace getTimeline(in:completion:) with the code given in Listing 4-2.

Listing 4-2. getTimeline(in:completion:) method that performs an API call by calling fetchOnThisDayData(with:)

```
func getTimeline(in context: Context, completion: @escaping
(Timeline<Entry>) -> Void) {
    // 1
    OnThisDayAPI.fetchOnThisDayData { widgetData in
    // 2
        let currentDate = Date()
    // 3
        let refreshDate = Calendar.current.date(byAdding:
        .day, value: 1, to: currentDate)!
    // 4
        let entry = WidgetEvent(date: currentDate, events:
        widgetData)
    // 5
        let timeline = Timeline(entries: [entry], policy:
        .after(refreshDate))
    // 6
        completion(timeline)
    }
}
```

In the code of Listing 4-2, the following things are happening:

1. The static fetchOnThisDayData(with:) method of the OnThisDayAPI struct is called.

2. As soon as the completion handler of
    fetchOnThisDayData(with:) returns the results
    as widgetData, the current date is stored in
    currentDate.

3. Now the date of the next day is stored in
    refreshDate. It will be used later to set up the
    widget's refresh policy.

4. Since a widget depends upon timeline entries to
    create a timeline, a WidgetEvent timeline entry
    is created and stored in entry. And the values
    of currentDate and widgetData, received as
    the response of the API call, are passed to the
    WidgetEvent constructor.

5. As there is at least one timeline entry, it's time to
    create a timeline. So, a timeline is created and stored
    in timeline by passing an array containing entry.
    Also, the refresh policy is set to make the widget
    request new timeline after refreshDate. In this way,
    the widget is set to refresh everyday.

Now, select the **OnThisDayWidgetExtension** scheme (if you haven't
selected it) and run the code to see your widgets fetching data from
Wikipedia's API. Right now, your widgets will display information about all
the events (and not an event of a certain category). Initially, the widget(s)
may take some time before loading updated data. So, have some patience
and enjoy your achievement. Your small, medium, and large widgets
should look similar to Figures 4-7, 4-8, and 4-9, respectively.

You have successfully given your widgets the capability to load
event information from an API. Well done! But events can lie in different
categories, and users may want information related to a particular event

category only. In the upcoming section, you will add the feature to allow users to configure your widgets to display information related only to a certain category.

Allowing Users to Configure Widgets

This section will be about making your widgets configurable. Right now, your widgets are displaying event information regardless of their categories. But maybe some users would love to configure their widgets in such a way that they get information only about a specific category of events. Maybe someone would like to keep track of birthdays of historical personalities, or maybe someone likes to get information about special historical events that took place. To serve that purpose, you can develop your widgets in such a way that users can select their preferred event category and configure them to show information related to that particular event category.

Now this is where `IntentConfiguration` comes into play. Till now, you have used `StaticConfiguration` only because you did not need to allow your users to configure widgets according to their preferences. If you do not remember where you had used `StaticConfiguration`, open the **OnThisDayWidget** folder. There, you will see a folder called **Widget**. Open it to find **OnThisDayWidget.swift**, which is the entry point of your widgets. This is where you have created a `StaticConfiguration`. In **OnThisDayWidget.swift**, you should see a block of code similar to Listing 4-3.

Listing 4-3. The StaticConfiguration in OnThisDayWidget.swift

```
var staticConfiguration: some WidgetConfiguration {
        StaticConfiguration(kind: kind, provider: Provider()) {
        entry in
            WidgetView(events: entry.events)
        }
        .supportedFamilies([.systemSmall, .systemMedium,
        .systemLarge])
        .configurationDisplayName("On This Day")
        .description("Events that occured this day.")
    }
```

You will change this configuration to IntentConfiguration and make some other changes in some time to make your widgets configurable. Now it's time to get to work by following the given steps.

Create and Configure a SiriKit Intent Definition File

Firstly, you will create an intent definition file since it will allow you to define customizable or configurable properties for your widgets. For creating that file and configuring it, follow the steps given as follows:

1. Right-click the **OnThisDayWidget** folder in your project and click **New File...**.

2. In the dialog box that appears, select **SiriKit Intent Definition File**, name it **EventCategory. intentdefinition**, and create the file. While creating the file, make sure that both **OnThisDayWidgetExtension** and **OnThisDay** targets are checked at the bottom of the dialog

box. If you do not check the **OnThisDay** target
while creating this file, your configuration options
(category selection field in your case) will not
appear in the configuration screen of your widgets.

3. Now, open **EventCategory.intentdefinition**.
Click the "+" icon at the bottom left of the intent
file, and from the list of options, click **New Intent**
(Figure 4-13).

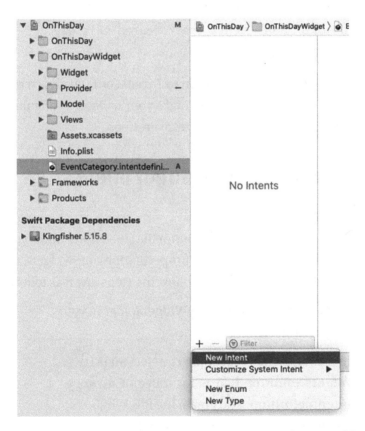

Figure 4-13. *Creating a new intent in the intent definition file*

4. Give your intent the name **EventCategory**. Then, go to the right side of the file and set the **Category** to **View**.

5. Since you are going to use the intent for widgets only, put a checkmark on **Intent is eligible for widgets** and remove checkmarks from **Intent is user-configurable in the Shortcuts app and Add to Siri** and **Intent is eligible for Siri Suggestions**.

6. Now, add a parameter named **categories** in the **Parameters** section by clicking the "+" button below it. The parameters added in the **Parameters** section are the configurable properties that users will see and interact with in the configuration screen of the widget. As you complete typing the name, you will see the display name set to **Categories**. The display name is displayed in the configuration screen of the widget (Figure 4-11).

7. Then change the type of the **categories** parameter to **Add Enum...** as you would like to display a list of selectable categories to the user in the widget configuration screen displayed in Figures 4-11 and 4-12. For your ease, this step is shown in Figure 4-14.

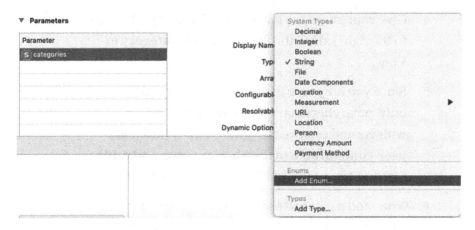

Figure 4-14. *Creating a parameter called "categories" and changing its "Type" to "Add Enum..."*

8. After clicking **Add Enum...**, a new screen is
    displayed that looks like Figure 4-15. Then, change
    the name of the enum to **Categories** by typing it in
    the item under the **ENUMS** header at the left.

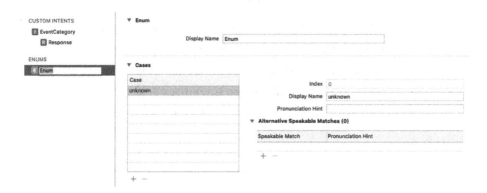

Figure 4-15. *The screen shown after clicking "Add Enum..."*

9. Now, go back to the **EventCategory** custom intent and select the **categories** parameter. Then, remove the checkmark from **Siri can ask for value when run**, as we do not want to work with Siri.

10. Again, open the **Categories** enum shown below the **ENUMS** header. Now it's time to add cases by clicking the "+" icon below the **Cases** section. Set the names of the cases to **all**, **births**, **deaths**, **events**, **holidays**, and **selected** and their display names to **All**, **Births**, **Deaths**, **Events**, **Holidays**, and **Selected**, respectively. These display names are shown to users in the configuration screen (Figure 4-12). If you have noticed the index of each case, you will see that the index of **unknown** is set as 0, and it cannot be modified. But, the indices of other cases are set in a numerical order, and Xcode allows you to modify them. At the end, your enum will look like Figure 4-16.

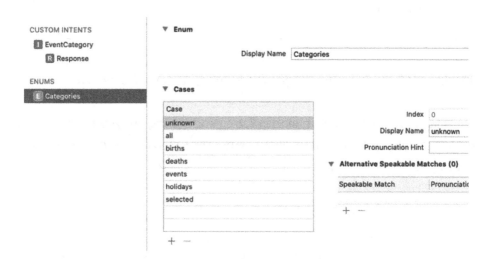

Figure 4-16. *The final look of the Categories enum*

11. Now for the final step, open the **EventCategory**
     custom intent and select the **categories** parameter
     in the **Parameters** section to see its configuration.
     Under the **Input** section at the right side of the
     window, set **Default Value** to **All** so that your widget
     displays information about all categories of events
     in case users do not ever configure your widgets
     to get information related to a certain category of
     events (Figure 4-17).

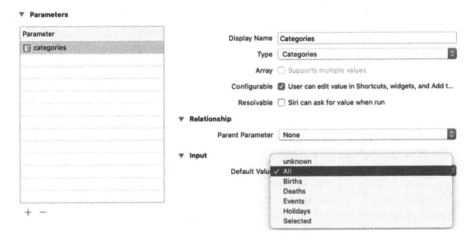

Figure 4-17. *Setting the "Default Value" of "categories" to "All."*

Like this, you have completed creating and setting up your intent
definition file. Congratulations! You are now one step closer to making
your widget configurable.

Switch to IntentConfiguration

As mentioned previously, you had used `StaticConfiguration` till now because there was no need to make your widgets user configurable. But now, you want to make them user configurable, and you have already completed the first step of the setup. Now, it's time to switch to `IntentConfiguration`. For that, you will have to follow the given steps:

1. Right-click the **Provider** folder of the **OnThisDayWidget** folder, click **New File…**, and create a new Swift file named **IntentProvider.swift**. Make sure the **OnThisDayWidgetExtension** target is checked at the bottom of the dialog box before creating the file.

Note   You could use the existing **Provider.swift** file instead of creating **IntentProvider.swift**, but for better clarity, we recommend you to create **IntentProvider.swift**.

---

2. Open the **IntentProvider.swift** file and replace the existing code content with the code given in Listing 4-4.

Listing 4-4. Creating IntentProvider that conforms to IntentTimelineProvider

```
import SwiftUI
import WidgetKit

struct IntentProvider: IntentTimelineProvider {

}
```

3. In Listing 4-4, a struct named `IntentProvider` that
    conforms to `IntentTimelineProvider` is created.
    As soon as you add the code, Xcode will ask if you
    want to add protocol stubs. Click **Fix** and add them
    to see two typealiases, `Entry` and `Intent`, added to
    the struct.

4. In the `IntentProvider` struct, replace the `type`
    placeholder of `Entry` with `WidgetEvent`, a timeline
    entry type. Also, replace the `type` placeholder of
    `Intent` with `EventCategoryIntent`. The name
    `EventCategoryIntent` was generated from the
    custom intent, `EventCategory`, you had previously
    created in your intent definition file, that is,
    EventCategory.intentdefinition.

Tip   While replacing the `type` placeholder of `Intent` with
`EventCategoryIntent` in `IntentProvider`, it would be a
better idea to type `EventCategoryIntent` yourself to check
if Xcode gives the autocompletion or not. It can help you verify if
`EventCategoryIntent` has been generated by Xcode or not.

Now your code should look similar to the code in Listing 4-5.

Listing 4-5. IntentProvider after adding Entry and Intent types

```
import SwiftUI
import WidgetKit

struct IntentProvider: IntentTimelineProvider {
  typealias Entry = WidgetEvent
  typealias Intent = EventCategoryIntent
}
```

5. Still Xcode must be asking you to add protocol stubs. Add them too to find `placeholder(in:)`, `getSnapshot (for:in:completion:)`, and `getTimeline(for:in: completion:)` methods generated.

6. For now, you can fill up those methods by copying and pasting code from the methods in **Provider. swift** to make `IntentProvider` look like Listing 4-6.

Note   Keep in mind that the methods in `IntentProvider` are different from those in `Provider`. `Provider` has methods like `getSnapshot(in:completion:)` and `getTimeline(in:completion:)`, but `IntentProvider` has methods like `getSnapshot(for:in:completion:)` and `getTimeline(for:in:completion:)`.

So, while copying code from `Provider`, make sure that you do not copy the whole methods but only the lines within the braces of those methods. For ease, you can copy the code from Listing 4-6.

Listing 4-6. IntentProvider after implementing required methods

```
import SwiftUI
import WidgetKit

struct IntentProvider: IntentTimelineProvider {
  typealias Entry = WidgetEvent

  typealias Intent = EventCategoryIntent
```

```swift
func placeholder(in context: Context) -> WidgetEvent {
  WidgetEvent(date: Date(), events: WidgetEventData.events)
}

func getSnapshot(for configuration: EventCategoryIntent, in
context: Context, completion: @escaping (WidgetEvent) ->
Void) {
  let entry = WidgetEvent(date: Date(), events:
  WidgetEventData.events)
  completion(entry)
}

func getTimeline(for configuration: EventCategoryIntent,
in context: Context, completion: @escaping
(Timeline<WidgetEvent>) -> Void) {
  OnThisDayAPI.fetchOnThisDayData { widgetData in
    let currentDate = Date()
    let refreshDate = Calendar.current.date(byAdding: .day,
    value: 1, to: currentDate)!
    let entry = WidgetEvent(date: currentDate, events:
    widgetData)
    let timeline = Timeline(entries: [entry], policy:
    .after(refreshDate))
    completion(timeline)
  }
}
}
```

7. Since it's necessary for the timeline entries in your widget to know the selected event category, you need to modify your timeline entry model. Navigate to **WidgetEventData.swift** in **Model** and add a new property, category, of the Categories

type to the WidgetEvent struct. Categories is the
enum that you had defined in **EventCategory.
intentdefinition**. Also, set its value to .all to make
it the default selected category. Now, WidgetEvent
should look similar to Listing 4-7.

Listing 4-7. WidgetEvent struct after adding the category property

```
struct WidgetEvent: TimelineEntry {
  var date: Date
  var events: [WidgetEventData]
  var category: Categories = .all
}
```

8.   Now go back to **IntentProvider.swift**. The
implementations of placeholder(in:) and
getSnapshot(for:in:completion:) do not
need to be modified, except that of getTimeline(
for:in:completion:).

The configuration parameter in getTimeline(for:
in:completion:) stores all the widget configuration
values set by users. Hence, it also holds the category
value set by users. This category value needs to be
passed to each timeline entry so that the widget can
fetch the event data related to a specific event category.
You can pass the category value to each timeline entry
by using the category property you just added in
WidgetEvent in step 7. If you see the implementation
of getTimeline(for:in:completion:), you can find
the line shown in Listing 4-8.

Listing 4-8. The line in getTimeline(for:in:completion:) that creates a WidgetEvent timeline entry

```
let entry = WidgetEvent(date: currentDate, events: widgetData)
```

> Listing 4-8 shows the line of code in getTimeline
> (for:in:completion:) that creates a WidgetEvent
> timeline entry and stores it into entry. Now, replace
> that line with the line given in Listing 4-9.

Listing 4-9. Creation of a WidgetEvent timeline entry that takes the category as an argument

```
let entry = WidgetEvent(date: currentDate, events:
widgetData, category: configuration.categories)
```

> Listing 4-9 creates a WidgetEvent timeline entry
> that takes the category from configuration data
> as an argument. This completes the setup of
> IntentProvider.

9. In this step, you will finally use the IntentProvider you just configured. Open **OnThisDayWidget. swift** in the **Widget** folder and replace the body of OnThisDayWidget with the code in Listing 4-10.

Listing 4-10. OnThisDayWidget's body using IntentConfiguration

```
var body: some WidgetConfiguration {
    IntentConfiguration(kind: kind,
                        intent: EventCategoryIntent.self,
                        provider: IntentProvider()) { entry in
        WidgetView(events: entry.events)
    }
    .supportedFamilies([.systemSmall, .systemMedium,
    .systemLarge])
```

```
    .configurationDisplayName("On This Day")
    .description("Events that occured this day.")
}
```

If you look at the code in Listing 4-10, you will see that the body of `OnThisDayWidget` has an `IntentConfiguration` initializer instead of a `StaticConfiguration` initializer. The only difference between those initializers is that `IntentConfiguration` takes an argument, `intent`, with the value, `EventCategoryIntent.self` (you had created this custom intent in `EventCategory. intentdefinition`), and another argument, `provider`, with an initializer of `IntentProvider`. All the other codes are identical to that of the `StaticConfiguration` initializer that was previously being used. Also, delete the `staticConfiguration` variable as you will not need it anymore.

Like this, you have completed switching to `IntentConfiguration` from `StaticConfiguration`. Now it's time to make the API call and display the result in the views.

Talk to the API and Display Fresh Information in Widgets

If you open **OnThisDayAPI.swift**, the file that contains the OnThisDayAPI struct responsible to perform API calls, and study its static fetchOnThisDayData(with:) method, you will see that no work has been done to fetch and return data according to a selected event category. It just performs an API call to Wikipedia's REST API endpoint, which returns data related to various categories of events under different keys. Then, the method stores those data of each and every category in a variable called response and returns it. Hence, currently, the method is returning only the results of the all category. Let's modify this method so that it is able to filter and return events lying in categories other than all too. Replace the fetchOnThisDayData(with:) method with the code given in Listing 4-11.

Listing 4-11. fetchOnThisDayData(for:completion:) method

```
static func fetchOnThisDayData(for type: Categories,
completion: @escaping ([WidgetEventData]?) -> Void) {
  guard let today = DateHelper.getDayAndMonthInNumbers(),
        let url = URL(string: "https://en.wikipedia.org/api/
        rest_v1/feed/onthisday/all/\(today.month)/\(today.
        day)") else { return }
  let task = URLSession.shared.dataTask(with: url) { data,
  response, _ in
    if let data = data,
       let response = response as? HTTPURLResponse,
       response.statusCode == 200 {
      do {
        let otdResponse = try JSONDecoder().decode(
        OTDResponse.self, from: data)
        var responses: [EventData] = []
        switch type {
        case .births: responses = otdResponse.births
        case .deaths: responses = otdResponse.deaths
        case .events: responses = otdResponse.events
        case .holidays: responses = otdResponse.holidays
        case .selected: responses = otdResponse.selected
        default: responses = otdResponse.selected
```

```
+ otdResponse.births + otdResponse.deaths + otdResponse.events
+ otdResponse.holidays
      }
      completion(responses.map({ WidgetEventData(text:
      $0.text) }))
    } catch {
      completion(nil)
      print("JSON Decoding Error.")
    }
  }
}
task.resume()
}
```

Listing 4-11 is the code that replaces the old fetchOnThisDayData(with:) method. This new method fetchOnThisDay Data(for:completion:), in addition to the completion handler, has a new parameter named for of type Categories. This for parameter plays an important role in filtering the data according to the selected category. It is visible in the switch case used in the code. A switch case is applied on the type variable (previously for variable), and only the results of a particular category are returned by the method as long as other categories, except the default category all, are selected. For example, if the selected type/category is births, the method will return only the data held by the births key of the API response.

Now build the code to see the locations affected by this change. The first location affected is **Provider.swift**. Since the struct in this file was being used by StaticConfiguration and now you are no longer using StaticConfiguration, delete **Provider.swift**. After that, the only affected area remaining will be **IntentProvider.swift**. Xcode must be saying, "Missing argument for parameter 'for' in call." Click **Fix** to make Xcode add the necessary argument for. And replace the placeholder with configuration.categories to fetch the selected category from your widget's configuration. Now your call to the fetchOnThisDayData(for: completion:) method in getTimeline(for:in:completion:) should look something like Listing 4-12.

Listing 4-12. fetchOnThisDayData(for:completion:) method after fetching categories from the widget's configuration

```
func getTimeline(for configuration: EventCategoryIntent, in
context: Context, completion: @escaping (Timeline<WidgetEvent>)
-> Void) {
    OnThisDayAPI.fetchOnThisDayData(for: configuration.
    categories) { widgetData in
      let currentDate = Date()
      let refreshDate = Calendar.current.date(byAdding: .day,
      value: 1, to: currentDate)!
      let entry = WidgetEvent(date: currentDate, events:
      widgetData, category: configuration.categories)
      let timeline = Timeline(entries: [entry], policy:
      .after(refreshDate))
      completion(timeline)
    }
}
```

Still, you must be seeing another error message from Xcode. This time, it must be saying, "Value of optional type '[WidgetEventData]?' must be unwrapped to a value of type '[WidgetEventData]'." To get rid of this, use guard-let to unwrap the optional widgetData value received from the fetchOnThisDayData(for:completion:) method's completion handler. After using guard-let, the function call of fetchOnThisDayData(for: completion:) in getTimeline(for:in:completion:) should look like Listing 4-13.

Listing 4-13. fetchOnThisDayData(for:completion:) method unwrapping widgetData using guard-let

```
func getTimeline(for configuration: EventCategoryIntent, in
context: Context, completion: @escaping (Timeline<WidgetEvent>)
-> Void) {
    OnThisDayAPI.fetchOnThisDayData(for: configuration.
    categories) { widgetData in
      guard let widgetData = widgetData else { return }
      let currentDate = Date()
      let refreshDate = Calendar.current.date(byAdding: .day,
      value: 1, to: currentDate)!
      let entry = WidgetEvent(date: currentDate, events:
      widgetData, category: configuration.categories)
      let timeline = Timeline(entries: [entry], policy:
      .after(refreshDate))
      completion(timeline)
    }
}
```

After using guard-let to unwrap widgetData as shown in Listing 4-13, the error message should be gone. Build your project to verify it.

Now there is one more thing remaining, that is, setting up the widget views to display the selected category. If you take a look at how the widgets look, you will see that there is a text that says, "200 births took place on JAN 20.", if the selected event category is births, the date is January 20, and the number of events in the births category is 200. So, let's set up the view.

Start setting up the view by adding the line of code given in Listing 4-14 in WidgetView, SmallWidgetView, MediumWidgetView, and LargeWidgetView.

Listing 4-14. Creating a variable "category" of Categories type

```
var category: Categories
```

As soon as you complete creating that variable in all views, you will see errors in the previews of SmallWidgetView, MediumWidgetView, and LargeWidgetView since the argument for parameter category has not been passed in the previews. Click **Fix** to add the category parameter and set the argument to .all. For example, in the case of SmallWidgetView, something like Listing 4-15 can be done.

Listing 4-15. Fixing the preview of SmallWidgetView by passing a category

```
struct SmallWidget_Previews: PreviewProvider {
    static var previews: some View {
      SmallWidgetView(eventCount: 5, category: .all)
            .previewContext(WidgetPreviewContext(family:
            .systemSmall))
    }
}
```

Pass a category argument in the previews of MediumWidgetView and LargeWidgetView to get rid of the error messages.

Now, if you build the project, you will still see more errors. This time, the errors are in **WidgetView.swift** since the initializers of SmallWidgetView, MediumWidgetView, and LargeWidgetView in the switch case have not been passed the category argument. Pass the category argument to make the body of your WidgetView look similar to Listing 4-16.

Listing 4-16. The body of WidgetView after passing a category to all widget families

```
@ViewBuilder
    var body: some View {
        switch family {
        case .systemSmall: SmallWidgetView(eventCount: events.
        count, category: category)
        case .systemMedium: MediumWidgetView(events: events,
        category: category)
        case .systemLarge: LargeWidgetView(events: events,
        category: category)
        default: EmptyView()
        }
    }
```

In Listing 4-16, the category variable of WidgetView is passed as an argument for the category parameters of all families of widget views.

Now, the error remains only in **OnThisDayWidget.swift**. Add the category parameter and pass entry.category as its argument in WidgetView's initializer to remove that error. After that, the body of OnThisDayWidget will look like Listing 4-17.

Listing 4-17. The body of OnThisDayWidget after passing a category to WidgetView's initializer

```
var body: some WidgetConfiguration {
    IntentConfiguration(kind: kind,
                        intent: EventCategoryIntent.self,
                        provider: IntentProvider()) { entry in
      WidgetView(events: entry.events, category: entry.category)
    }
```

```
    .supportedFamilies([.systemSmall, .systemMedium,
    .systemLarge])
    .configurationDisplayName("On This Day")
    .description("Events that occured this day.")
}
```

If you have done everything mentioned earlier but are unable to understand what happened, let us explain. You passed the selected category received from the entry variable of the completion handler of the IntentConfiguration initializer in OnThisDayWidget, which is the entry point of your widget, to WidgetView, your main widget view. Then, from WidgetView, category was further passed to SmallWidgetView, MediumWidgetView, and LargeWidgetView.

Now, SmallWidgetView, MediumWidgetView, and LargeWidgetView are ready to use their category variables to display the selected category in the widgets. But before that, let's do some necessary setup.

Create a new folder **Intent** and move **EventCategory.intentdefinition** into that folder. Now, create a new Swift file in the **Intent** folder and name it **CategoriesExtension.swift**. Make sure that **OnThisDay** and **OnThisDayWidgetExtension** targets are selected while creating that file. Now, copy the code given in Listing 4-18 and paste it in **CategoriesExtension.swift**.

Listing 4-18. Creating an extension of Categories

```
extension Categories {
  var detail: String {
    switch self {
    case .births: return "births"
    case .all: return "historic events"
    case .events: return "events"
    case .deaths: return "deaths"
    case .holidays: return "holidays"
```

```
    case .selected: return "special events"
    default: return "historic events"
    }
  }
}
```

In Listing 4-18, an extension of Categories is created. It contains a detail variable of String type. Using the switch case, it returns the string to be displayed in the widgets according to the selected category.

Now, in SmallWidgetView, MediumWidgetView, and LargeWidgetView, search for the text Text("events") and replace it with Text(category. detail) so that the category of the selected event is displayed on the widget.

Finally, it's time to test your widgets!

Time to Put Your Widgets to the Test!

In your simulator or device, uninstall any existing installation of **OnThisDay** and remove any existing widget of **OnThisDay**. Then, select and run the **OnThisDay** target first to install it on your simulator or device. After that, select and run the **OnThisDayWidgetExtension** target to install the widgets. After the widgets are shown in the homescreen, try going to its configuration screen and selecting a different category. You can refer to Figures 4-10, 4-11, and 4-12. After selecting a new category, the information related to the events of that particular category should show up in your widget.

Well done! You have successfully made your widgets user configurable.

Navigating to the Relevant Screens of the App Through Tap Targets

Did you try tapping the different elements of your widgets you created in the previous section? The app must be launching and showing its homescreen no matter where you tap in your widgets. This should be changed as your widget is not your app icon, but way more than that. And it is also suggested in the Human Interface Guidelines to create such a widget, which when tapped should launch the app to show the screen containing the details and actions useful and relevant to the widget's content.

So, in this section, you will define tap targets that, when tapped, will use deep links to make navigation to various relevant screens of your app possible.

Note   Deep linking is a technique with which you can make a link or URL not only open your app but also automatically navigate to the desired location of your app. It is very popular these days and has been adopted by various companies and organizations in their apps and services.

A nice example of a company utilizing the power of deep linking is Medium. If you open Medium's website and read an article in your phone's browser, you will see a button that says, "Open in app" at the top of the page. After tapping that button, if you are using an iOS device and do not have the Medium app installed, the App Store will launch in your device and display the installation page of the Medium app. But if you are using an iOS device with the Medium app installed, it will launch and take you to the same article you were reading, inside the app. That's some awesome deep linking magic!

For example, if you take a look at your medium-sized widget (Figure 4-18), you will see that there are various areas and elements which can be used as tap targets to make navigation to the screens containing the details and actions relevant to the tap targets' content possible. The potential tap targets are highlighted using rectangles with red borders in Figure 4-18.

Figure 4-18. *Highlighting the elements which can be made tappable*

In Figure 4-18, the first potential tap target is the area that says, "207 births took place on JAN 20." As the currently selected category of events is **Births,** you can make that area tappable to navigate users to the app's homescreen that displays only the events lying in the **Births** category.

Also, you can see that there are a couple of birth events listed at the right side of the widget. So, you can define tap targets of each event in the list to directly navigate users to the detail screen of that tapped event. Hence, this time, the screen that will be displayed will not be the homescreen, but the detail screen with the content and actions relevant to the event that was tapped in the widget. For example, in Figure 4-18, if users tap the event that says, "Calum Chambers, English footballer," then users should see the detail screen containing the details about "Calum Chambers."

There is one more potential tap target that informs users that there are more events that could not be listed in the widget. In Figure 4-18, it says, "205 more." Therefore, it's obvious that by tapping it, users will expect to go to the app's homescreen that displays all the events lying in the **Births** category.

Since the large-sized widget is similar to the medium-sized widget, the potential tap targets are the same.

But in the case of a small-sized widget, WidgetKit allows you to define only a single tap target, as it has little space and can accommodate less content. So, in your small widget, you can define a tap target that takes users to the homescreen that displays a list of events lying in the selected category.

Addition of Tap Target in Small Widget

In small widgets, you can add a tap target using the widgetURL(_:) method. It is an instance method of View, and it sets the URL to open in the app when users tap a widget. Another View method onOpenURL(perform:) detects if any deep link is trying to open the app, and that is where you perform necessary operations to make navigation to different screens possible. So, in the case of small widgets, these two methods play the key role to make navigation possible.

Now let's set things up!

The widgetURL(_:) method takes a URL as an argument in order to set that URL for opening the app when its small widget is tapped. So, it is necessary to create a URL for the widgetURL(_:) method (which you will implement later). But what will you use to generate a URL? You will surely need a name or some other string for that. What about using the name of the selected category itself? That will be a nice way since you will get both the URL and the selected category value which you will use in the app's homescreen to display the events lying in that category. Now, follow the given steps to develop a mechanism for generating a URL:

1. Open **CategoriesExtension.swift** from the **Intent** folder of **OnThisDayWidget**.

2. In the extension of Categories, copy the code of Listing 4-19 and paste it there to define a property, eventType, of type EventType.

Listing 4-19. Creating an eventType property in the Categories extension

```
var eventType: EventType {
    switch self {
    case .unknown, .all: return .all
    case .births: return .births
    case .deaths: return .deaths
    case .events: return .events
    case .holidays: return .holidays
    case .selected: return .selected
    }
}
```

eventType was created in the Categories extension because you need to generate a String from the selected category of Categories type for creating a URL. Since EventType conforms to String and its rawValue property can be accessed to get the string of the selected category, you created eventType to map all the cases of Categories with EventType and get the string rawValue.

3. After that, open **SmallWidgetView.swift** in the
   Views folder of the **OnThisDayWidget** folder.

4. Replace the body of SmallWidgetView with the code
   given in Listing 4-20.

Listing 4-20. The body of SmallWidgetView after adding
widgetURL(_:)

```
var body: some View {
    HStack {
        VStack(alignment: .leading) {
          Text(eventCount.description)
            .font(.system(size: 40,
                            weight: .medium))
            .foregroundColor(.red)
          Text(category.detail)
            .font(.body)
          Text("took place on")
            .font(.body)
          Text(DateHelper.today + ".")
            .font(.headline)
        }
        Spacer()
      }
    .padding([.leading, .top, .bottom])
    .widgetURL(URL(string: category.eventType.rawValue))
  }
```

In Listing 4-20, the widgetURL(_:) method is
called by passing a URL created using the rawValue
property of the eventType property of category as
an argument.

5. Open **HomeView.swift** from the **Views** folder
    of **OnThisDay**. In HomeView, create a method,
    handleLinks(for:), to handle deep linking and
    copy the code in Listing 4-21 and paste it there.

Listing 4-21. Implementation of handleLinks(for:)

```swift
func handleLinks(for url: URL) {
    if let type = EventType(rawValue: url.absoluteString) {
      self.type = type
  }
}
```

In Listing 4-21, the handleLinks(for:) method is
implemented. The absoluteString[3] property of
url is accessed to get its string value, and the string
value is passed to the EventType initializer that
takes rawValue as an argument and tries to convert
it to an EventType case. If a valid EventType case is
generated, then it is stored in the type variable. At
last, the type variable of HomeView is set to the value
of the type variable of the if-let condition. Here,
the type variable of HomeView is a @State variable
that stores the selected event category/event type
and displays the events accordingly.

6. Now, go to the body of HomeView. This is where
    you will call onOpenURL(perform:) to detect
    if a deep link is trying to launch your app.

---

[3]https://developer.apple.com/documentation/foundation/
nsurl/1409868-absolutestring

Below the onAppear(perform:) function call in
the body of HomeView, add the function call to
onOpenURL(perform:) and make the changes
shown in Listing 4-22.

Listing 4-22. HomeView's body after calling onOpenURL(perform:)

```
var body: some View {
    NavigationView {
        // Some lines of code have been removed to make
            viewing easier
    }
// Some lines of code have been removed to make viewing easier
    .onAppear(perform: initiateDataFetch)
    .onOpenURL { url in
      handleLinks(for: url)
    }
}
```

In Listing 4-22, the onOpenURL(perform:) method
is called, whose completion handler gives a
parameter, url. That parameter is passed to
handleLinks(for:), which performs the work of
filtering the data and setting up the view to display
events related to the selected event category/type.

___

Note   The call to onOpenURL(perform:) is performed in the body
of HomeView because HomeView is the main view that gets loaded
from the entry point of the app, that is, OnThisDayApp. You will see
it if you open the **OnThisDayApp.swift** file in the **OnThisDay** folder.

However, you could have called onOpenURL(perform:) from the
OnThisDayApp struct using the instance of HomeView. But due to the
availability of the data needed for performing necessary operations,
you called it from the body of HomeView.

SwiftUI has given you the freedom to call onOpenURL(perform:)
from any of these locations according to your preference and ease.

Now, build and run the project. Try changing the selected category
of the events by long pressing the small widget, tapping **Edit Widget**, and
modifying the value of the **Categories** field. Then, wait for the widget
display information about the events of the selected category. After the
fresh information is displayed in the widget, tap the widget to see the
homescreen of the app displaying the list of events related to the selected
category.

Well done! You have successfully added a tap target in your small
widget and utilized the power of deep linking to make your app display
relevant information.

Addition of Tap Target in Medium Widget

As shown in Figure 4-18, you can have multiple tap targets in your medium
and large widgets. So, in this section, you will add tap targets in your
medium widget.

In the medium widget, there are three regions where you can add tap
targets. Open and preview MediumWidgetView so that it becomes easier for
you to understand.

The first region/view is eventCountView that displays the number of
events that took place on a particular date. It resembles your small widget.

The next region is the one where two events are listed. The
eventDetail(with:) method is responsible to display that region. Each of
them can have its own tap target that takes users to its detail screen.

And below that region, there is a todayEvents view that displays the number of remaining events that could not be accommodated in the widget view, but are displayed when the app is launched.

You must have noticed that the only region which will have a tap target that will perform a different function is the eventDetail(with:) method. Otherwise, no matter where you tap in the medium widget, users are supposed to be taken to the app's homescreen displaying a list of events related to the currently selected category. So, like in your small widget, you can call widgetURL(_:) from one of your views of your medium widget. Later, to add a tap target in the eventDetail(with:) method, you will use some other way than widgetURL(_:).

Since you have already performed the setup necessary to handle deep links during the "Addition of Tap Target in Small Widget" (step 5 onwards), now you can simply call widgetURL(_:) from any view among eventCountView and todayEvents to make things work. Let's call widgetURL(_:) from eventCountView. Listing 4-23 shows the addition of the call to widgetURL(_:) in eventCountView.

Listing 4-23. Calling widgetURL(_:) from eventCountView

```
var eventCountView: some View {
  HStack {
    VStack(alignment: .leading) {
      Text(events.count.description)
        .font(.system(size: 40,
                      weight: .medium))
        .foregroundColor(.red)
      Text(category.detail)
        .font(.body)
      Text("took place on")
        .font(.body)
```

```
        Text(DateHelper.today + ".")
            .font(.headline)
        }
    }
    .padding(.trailing)
    .widgetURL(URL(string: category.eventType.rawValue))
}
```

In Listing 4-23, `widgetURL(_:)` was called in `eventCountView` by passing the URL created using the string generated by accessing the `rawValue` property of the `eventType` property of `category`, which is the selected category.

After adding the code in Listing 4-23, build and run the widget. Now, if you tap anywhere in the medium widget, you will get taken to the app's homescreen that lists the events related to the selected category.

However, if you remember, the region that displays brief information about two events at the right side of the widget is supposed to take users to their detail screens in the app to provide more relevant information. It's time to set it up.

In the case of the small widget, all you needed for the app to display the list of events of a selected category was the name of the selected category itself. And you created a URL using that category name and set it via `widgetURL(_:)`. When the widget was tapped, `onOpenURL(perform:)` would detect the deep link and the app would get launched and the homescreen with the list was displayed.

But you need a different mechanism to handle the case when an event is tapped in the medium (or large) widget, and the app should launch to open the detail screen of that particular event. Unlike in the small widget, here, you require both the event information (which will be used for the detail screen) and the selected category (which will be used to display the list of events of that particular category when users decide to go back to the app's homescreen).

As you will use deep linking for this case too, you will surely have to create a URL. So, why not generate a URL that will not only contain the selected category but also the text of the event? And to make the app sure about the screen it should navigate to when that particular deep link is detected, why not include some information about that screen too? It may not be very useful currently, but in scenarios where your app may have deep links for navigating to various screens, it can surely come handy.

So, let's create a mechanism that generates the URL containing the information about the selected category, the text of the event, and the name of the screen the app should navigate to:

1. In the **OnThisDayWidget** folder, create a new folder, **Constants**.

2. In **Constants**, create a new Swift file named **LinkConstants.swift**. While creating that file, make sure both **OnThisDay** and **OnThisDayWidgetExtension** targets are checked.

3. Copy the code in Listing 4-24 and paste it in **LinkConstants.swift**.

Listing 4-24. Creating a LinkConstants struct

```
struct LinkConstants {
  // a
  static let detailScheme = "detail"
  // b
  static func detail(with text: String, category: Categories)
  -> URL? {
    // c
    let queryItem = URLQueryItem(name: "text", value: text)
```

```
// d
var urlComponents = URLComponents()
urlComponents.scheme = Self.detailScheme
urlComponents.host = category.eventType.rawValue
urlComponents.queryItems = [queryItem]
// e
if let url = urlComponents.url {
  return url
}
return nil
  }
}
```

In Listing 4-24, the LinkConstants struct is created, and the following things take place in it:

a. A static property, detailScheme, is defined, and its value is set to "detail". You will use this property to let the app know that the deep link wants it to navigate to the detail screen of an event.

b. A static detail(with:category:) method is created. It is where your URL will be generated.

c. A URLQueryItem with its name parameter, text, and its value parameter set to the text received as an argument from detail(with:category:) is defined and stored in queryItem.

d. By creating an instance of URLComponents and storing it in urlComponents, the work of creating a URL is started here. The scheme is set to detailScheme, the host is set to the string form

95

of category, and queryItems is set to an array
containing the queryItem variable you created
in step "a."

e. Using if-let, it is checked if a valid URL
has been generated or not. If a valid URL is
generated, it is stored in url and returned.
Else, the method returns nil. A sample
of the URL that is created is detail://
births?text=Cory%20Paix,%20Australian%20
rugby%20league%20player.

In this way, you have developed a mechanism to generate URLs using
the selected category, the text of the event, and the destination screen's
name.

Now, let's use the detail(with:category:) method you just created in
LinkConstants and also set up the view of the medium widget for enabling
navigation:

1. Open MediumWidgetView and replace todayEvents
with the code given in Listing 4-25.

Listing 4-25. todayEvents with the Link view

```
var todayEvents: some View {
    VStack(spacing: 0) {
        ForEach(events.prefix(2)) { event in
            // a
            if let url = LinkConstants.detail(with: event.text,
            category: category) {
                Link(destination: url, label: {
                    eventDetail(with: event)
                })
```

```
    } else {
      eventDetail(with: event)
    }
  }
  if events.count > 2 {
    HStack {
      Spacer()
      Text("\(events.count - 2) more")
        .font(.footnote)
        .padding(.trailing)
        .padding(.bottom, 8)
    }
  }
}
}
```

In Listing 4-25, a URL is generated by using the static detail(with:category:) method of LinkConstants and passing the text of the current iteration of events, that is, event, and the currently selected category, that is, category. If detail(with:category:) returns a valid URL, it is stored in url, and a Link view with its destination set to url and label set to the eventDetail(with:) method is created. Hence, the views that display brief information about events become tappable links to the URLs you generate. If detail(with:category:) does not generate a valid URL, just the view generated by the eventDetail(with:) method is displayed.

Tip   You can check if the Link view is working or not by setting
a breakpoint inside the onOpenURL(perform:) method in
HomeView. Then, build and run the project and add the medium
widget in your simulator or device's homescreen. After the updated
information gets loaded in the widget, tap on any event and your
app will launch, and the breakpoint will pause the execution inside
onOpenURL(perform:). Now check the deep link URL that passed
by typing po url in Xcode's **Debug Console**. If the URL that is
printed contains the data related to the event that you had tapped, it
can be concluded that the Link view is working.

2.   Open HomeView and define two State variables,
     deepLinkEvent of EventData? type and
     deepLinkActive of Bool type. Listing 4-26 shows the
     code that does it.

Listing 4-26.   Defining deepLinkEvent and deepLinkActive

```
@State var deepLinkEvent: EventData?
@State var deepLinkActive: Bool = false
```

The deepLinkEvent variable defined in Listing 4-26
will be used later to store the data of the event
that was tapped in the widget. Likewise, the
deepLinkActive variable declared in Listing 4-26 will
be used to activate/deactivate the NavigationLink
responsible for navigation to an event's detail screen.
You will add it later.

3. Let's create a method handleLinkForDetail(with:) in HomeView to handle operations related only to the navigation to an event's detail screen when a deep link is detected. Do it using the code given in Listing 4-27.

Listing 4-27. Creating handleLinkForDetail(with:)

```
func handleLinkForDetail(with url: URL) {
    // a
    guard let urlScheme = url.scheme,
        urlScheme == LinkConstants.detailScheme else {
        return }
    // b
    guard let urlType = url.host else { return }
    // c
    type = EventType(rawValue: urlType)!
    // d
    if let firstElement = url.queryParams.first {
        for eventType in otdViewModel.events {
            for event in eventType.value where event.text
            == firstElement.value {
                deepLinkEvent = event
                deepLinkActive = true
            }
        }
    }
}
```

In Listing 4-27, the following things are happening:

a. handleLinkForDetail(with:) receives a URL as an argument and stores it in url. Using guard-let, it is checked if url contains a scheme or not. If a scheme is present, it is stored in urlScheme, and a check is performed if urlScheme matches with LinkConstants.detailScheme (whose value is "detail") or not. This helps to verify if the deep link is meant to make the app navigate to a detail screen or not (we had talked about this in the step "a" of the explanation of Listing 4-24). Otherwise, the method will return and do nothing.

b. In this step, it is checked if url contains a host or not. If it contains a host, it is stored in urlType; otherwise, the method will return and do nothing. You have set up the URL in such a way that urlType will contain the string value of the selected event category.

c. Now, the value of urlType is passed to the EventType initializer to convert it into an EventType case. Since you can be sure that a String that can be converted into an EventType case has been passed, you can force-unwrap the result using the bang operator (!) and store it in type that stores the selected event category/event type and displays the events accordingly.

d. In this step, only the first query parameter passed in url is extracted using if-let, as you had passed only one query parameter containing the text of the event.

Now since firstElement contains the text of the event tapped, you can match it with the texts of the events variable of otdViewModel to find out the event data of that tapped event. These event data can then be used to initiate navigation to the detail page of the tapped event. The events variable is where the app stores all the events after fetching them using the API.

So, a for loop is run through the events variable of otdViewModel, setting the iteration variable to eventType. Again, another for loop is run through eventType.value to find out the text of the event that matches with the text of firstElement. As soon as an event is found, its value is stored in deepLinkEvent, which will make the value available throughout HomeView. And the deepLinkActive flag is set to true as it is verified that this is a valid deep link operation to navigate to the detail page.

4. Now it's time to call the handleLinkForDetail(with:) method you just created. Since the operations related to deep linking are mainly handled by the handleLinks(for:) method in HomeView, go there and replace it using the code in Listing 4-28 to give handleLinks(for:) some more responsibilities.

Listing 4-28. handleLinks(for:) with added responsibilities

```
func handleLinks(for url: URL) {
    deepLinkEvent = nil
    deepLinkActive = false
    if let type = EventType(rawValue: url.absoluteString) {
        self.type = type
    } else {
        handleLinkForDetail(with: url)
    }
}
```

Listing 4-28 contains the updated version of the handleLinks(for:) method. No matter what url is received, initially, deepLinkEvent is set to nil and deepLinkActive is set to false. Then, if url contains a String that can be converted into an EventType case, it is stored in the type variable. After that, the value of the type variable is stored in the type variable of HomeView, which is responsible to set the selected event category/event type and display the event list accordingly in the homescreen. You had previously used this condition for the small widget and for some portion of the medium widget.

But if url does not contain such a String, then it is deduced that it is time to handle the deep link for navigating to the detail screen of an event. Hence, in the else condition, handleLinkForDetail(with: url) is called.

5.   Now, the last thing remaining is to create a NavigationLink that gets activated and deactivated according to the deepLinkActive state variable of HomeView. When it gets activated, the app automatically navigates to the detail screen of an event. For that, create a variable named navigateToDetail by using the code given in Listing 4-29.

Listing 4-29. Defining the navigateToDetail variable

```
var navigateToDetail: some View {
        return self.deepLinkEvent.map({ event in
            NavigationLink(destination: DetailView(event:
            event), isActive: $deepLinkActive) {
                EmptyView()
            }.hidden()
        })
    }
```

In Listing 4-29, the navigateToDetail variable is created, whose function is to return some View. It first checks if a deepLinkEvent value is available or not by running map, and if the value exists, a NavigationLink with its destination set to DetailView, along with event data, and its isActive parameter set to $deepLinkActive, is created. Here, the "$" sign before deepLinkActive indicates that it is a binding. So, if there occurs any kind of change in deepLinkActive's value, then the whole body of HomeView automatically gets reloaded, and hence if deepLinkActive's value becomes true, the NavigationLink navigates to its destination, that is,

DetailView. Also, the label of NavigationLink is an EmptyView() and the whole NavigationLink is hidden() as you do not want it to be visible anywhere on screen but just want it to work.

6.   For a NavigationLink to work, it must be wrapped inside a NavigationView. So, the last step would be to somehow wrap navigateToDetail, which stores your NavigationLink, to the NavigationView in the body of HomeView. So, make navigateToDetail the background of the List wrapped by NavigationView in the body of HomeView. It is shown in Listing 4-30.

Listing 4-30. Setting navigateToDetail as the background of List in the body of HomeView

```
var body: some View {
    NavigationView {
        List {
            if type == .all {
                eventListWhenAllChecked
            } else {
                Group { eventView(for: type) }
            }
        }
        .background(navigateToDetail)
        .navigationTitle("On This Day")
        .navigationBarItems(leading: Text("\(today?.month ??
        "JANUARY") \(today?.day ?? 1)")
            .fontWeight(.semibold)
            .font(.body)
```

```
                .foregroundColor(.red),
                trailing: TrailingNavView(homeView: self))
    }

    .alert(isPresented: $isAlertDisplayed,
            content: {
                Alert(title: Text("Oops!"),
                        message: Text("An error occured. Please
                        try reloading the data."),
                        dismissButton: .cancel(Text("OK")))
            })

    .onAppear(perform: initiateDataFetch)
    .onOpenURL { url in
        handleLinks(for: url)
    }
}
```

If you see in Listing 4-30, exactly after the closing brace of List, .background(navigateToDetail) has been added to make navigateToDetail its background. In this way, you have successfully wrapped the NavigationLink stored by navigateToDetail in the NavigationView of HomeView's body.

7. Finally, build and run the project and tap any event of the medium-sized widget to see the app launching and automatically navigating to the detail page of that particular event. If you tap the **Back** button, you will see the list of events related to the selected category only, in the homescreen of the app.

With this, you have completed adding a tap target in your medium widget. Now, the only widget where you have not set up tap targets is the large widget. You will do that in the upcoming section.

Addition of Tap Target in Large Widget

In the previous sections, you have already performed the setup necessary to create and handle deep links. That makes adding tap targets in your large widget easier. The only file you will modify now is LargeWidgetView to make tap targets in it work.

As LargeWidgetView is quite similar to MediumWidgetView, the first thing you can do is call the widgetURL(_:) method. This will create a tap target throughout the view that will make navigation to the app's homescreen that displays a list of events of the selected category. Replace the body of LargeWidgetView with the code given in Listing 4-31.

Listing 4-31. Calling widgetURL(_:) from LargeWidgetView's body

```
var body: some View {
        VStack(alignment: .leading, spacing: 0) {
            today
            Divider().padding(.vertical, 4)
            count
            todayEvents
            Spacer()
        }
        .padding(8)
        .widgetURL(URL(string: category.eventType.rawValue))
    }
```

Listing 4-31 modifies the body of LargeWidgetView by adding a call to widgetURL(_:). The URL passed as an argument is created by using the String rawValue of the eventType property of category. Since you have set up everything to handle this deep link, if you build and run the project and you tap anywhere in the large widget, the app will launch and display a list of events of the selected category.

Now to add the feature to navigate to the detail screen of an event listed in the widget, you have to make modifications in todayEvents. Firstly, create a method eventDetail(with:) in LargeWidgetView by using the code given in Listing 4-32.

Listing 4-32. Creating eventDetail(with:)

```
func eventDetail(with event: WidgetEventData) -> some View {}
```

Listing 4-32 creates an eventDetail(with:) method that returns some View. Now, go to todayEvents and cut its HStack (everything inside the ForEach loop), and paste it in eventDetail(with:) to make it look like the code given in Listing 4-33.

Listing 4-33. Adding code to eventDetail(with:)

```
func eventDetail(with event: WidgetEventData) -> some View {
    HStack(spacing: 0) {
      Color.init(UIColor.systemYellow)
        .frame(width: 4)
        .padding(.vertical, 12)
      VStack {
        Text("\(event.text)")
          .font(.caption)
          .padding(.trailing, 8)
          .frame(maxWidth: .infinity, alignment: .leading)
      }.padding(8)
    }
  }
```

Listing 4-33 creates an eventDetail(with:) method that returns an HStack. If you look at the code of todayEvents now, you will see only the code shown in Listing 4-34.

Listing 4-34. The remnants of todayEvents

```
var todayEvents: some View {
      VStack(spacing: 0) {
          ForEach(events.prefix(3)) { event in
            // HStack was here
          }
          if events.count > 3 {
             HStack() {
                  Spacer()
                  Text("\(events.count - 3) more")
                      .font(.footnote)
                      .padding(.trailing)
             }
          }
      }
   }
```

The line where HStack existed previously has been marked with the comment, // HStack was here, in Listing 4-34. Now, replace the line that says // HStack was here with the code given in Listing 4-35.

Listing 4-35. The code that replaces the HStack

```
if let url = LinkConstants.detail(with: event.text, category:
category) {
                Link(destination: url) {
                  eventDetail(with: event)
                }
              } else {
                eventDetail(with: event)
              }
```

You had used the code in Listing 4-35 in MediumWidgetView too. The given code checks if a valid URL has been generated or not by passing event.text and category to the LinkConstants. detail(with:category:) method and by unwrapping the value returned by that method using an if-let. If a valid URL is generated, it is stored in url, and a Link with destination set to url wraps the call to eventDetail(with:) that is responsible to generate the HStack that displays the event details. Otherwise, only the eventDetail(with:) method is called.

Now, if you run the project and test your large widget, you will see that if you tap on any event, you get taken to its detail screen. And if you tap **Back** from a detail screen, the app displays the homescreen listing the events of the selected category.

In this way, you have successfully added tap targets in your large widget. Well done!

Summary

And you made it! In this chapter, you learned how you can make your widgets configurable and interactive to make your widgets more user-friendly. You used `IntentConfiguration` to make your widgets configurable, added tap targets in them, and used deep links to make navigation to the different screens of your app possible. In case of any confusion, do check out the final version of the code by opening the final project folder named **OnThisDayFinal** in **OnThisDay.zip**.

This chapter taught how you can provide hard-coded data to your widget's configuration. In the upcoming chapter, you will move a level ahead and provide dynamic data (fetched from an API) to your widget's configuration and make your widget even more powerful. Sounds exciting enough? Just keep going forward!

CHAPTER 5

Fetching Remote Configuration Options for Widgets

If you have made it to this chapter of the book, then till now you have gained an idea about how you can develop widgets of different sizes that not only display static data but also have the capability to fetch fresh data from a server at a specified interval. Also, you have learned how you can add tap targets to your widgets and also make your widgets configurable.

By following the procedure given in the previous chapter, you developed widgets that offered users a list of hard-coded configuration options, using which they configured their widgets. To be more specific, in the **OnThisDay** app's widgets, users could select a category of events from the widgets' configuration screen and, hence, make the widgets display event information related only to that particular category. You hard-coded all those categories which users could choose from. That is where the difference between that chapter and this chapter lies.

In this chapter, you will learn how you can fetch data from a server so that you can use those data as configuration options for the parameter in your configurable widgets. If you apply what you learned in this chapter to the **OnThisDay** app, you will be able to replace the category options you had previously hard-coded, with dynamic category options fetched from a server.

© Sagun Raj Lage and Prakshapan Shrestha 2021
S. R. Lage and P. Shrestha, *Getting Started with WidgetKit*,
https://doi.org/10.1007/978-1-4842-7042-4_5

Now, we understand that you must have been fed up with working on the same app for a long time. So, in this chapter, you will work in a new app, **TwitterTrends** (our friends who love Twitter are gonna enjoy this).

Getting Started

To begin working on TwitterTrends, unzip the file named **TwitterTrends.zip**, and from the **TwitterTrendsStarter** folder, open **TwitterTrends.xcodeproj**. As this project needs to use Twitter's API endpoints, it is necessary to generate a bearer token. You have to pass that bearer token in the header of each request/API call, and Twitter checks that bearer token for authentication. If a valid bearer token is passed, Twitter sends a response with the data you request. Otherwise, Twitter will not give you access.

If you already own a Twitter Developer Account, you should be able to generate your own bearer token. But in case you do not own a developer account, you will first have to apply for it from Twitter's developer account page.[1] Generally, it takes a day or two, or sometimes even more, for Twitter to review your application.

If your Twitter Developer Account is ready to use, generate your own bearer token by going through the article at this link.[2] Then, open **TwitterTrendsAPI.swift** in the **TwitterTrends** folder of the project and replace the string that says, "Your bearer token here," with your bearer token string. Finally, you are ready to run the app.

Now, select the **TwitterTrends** scheme and run the project to see a screen similar to the screenshot shown in Figure 5-1.

---

[1]https://developer.twitter.com/en/apply-for-access
[2]https://developer.twitter.com/en/docs/authentication/oauth-2-0/
 bearer-tokens

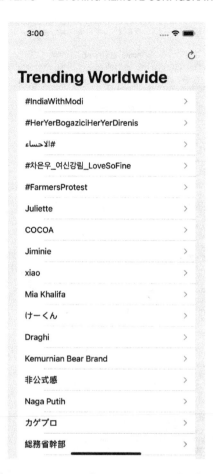

Figure 5-1. *The homescreen of TwitterTrends displaying a list of trends trending worldwide on Twitter*

Figure 5-1 shows the TwitterTrends app's homescreen displaying a list of top trends trending worldwide on Twitter. TwitterTrends does this by making use of Twitter's **GET trends/place**[3] API endpoint. If you play with the app, you will see that you can tap each trend to get taken to a screen that displays tweets related to that trend (Figure 5-2).

---

[3]https://developer.twitter.com/en/docs/twitter-api/v1/trends/ trends-for-location/api-reference/get-trends-place

Figure 5-2. *TwitterTrends displaying a list of tweets about the trend "#FarmersProtest"*

Figure 5-2 shows the screen with a list of tweets which was shown after the **#FarmersProtest** trend was tapped in TwitterTrends' homescreen. The list of tweets has been fetched by using Twitter's **GET search/tweets**[4] API endpoint.

---

[4]https://developer.twitter.com/en/docs/twitter-api/v1/tweets/search/
api-reference/get-search-tweets

To sum up, TwitterTrends lets users know about the top Twitter trends and also fetches the tweets related to those trends. But wait, did you check out the widget of TwitterTrends? TwitterTrends has a large widget (Figure 5-3) that displays the tweets related to the first trend of the array returned as a response by Twitter's **GET trends/place** API endpoint.

Figure 5-3. *Large-sized widget of TwitterTrends*

In Figure 5-3, you can see how the large widget of TwitterTrends looks. The large widget is the only widget family that TwitterTrends has. At the top of the widget, the name of the trend is displayed. Below that, the tweets related to that trend are listed, along with some more information about each tweet. If there are more than three tweets, a Text that displays the number of tweets that could not be accommodated in the widget is shown.

Right now, if you try to edit the widget and configure it, you will see that there exists no option to do that. But in the upcoming sections, you will make your app configurable (Figure 5-4). Users will be able to choose a trend from a list of trends fetched from Twitter's API endpoint (and not a list of hard-coded trends), and the widget will then display tweets related to that trend. This is what makes this chapter different from the previous one – fetching configuration options from a server and not hard-coding them.

Figure 5-4. *The configuration screen of TwitterTrends' widget*

Figure 5-4 displays the configuration screen of TwitterTrends' widget that you will develop in the upcoming sections. The configuration screen consists of a parameter, **Selected Trend**, which is currently asking users to **Choose** a trend since no trend has been selected yet. After tapping **Choose**, users will see a screen that lists the Twitter trends trending worldwide (Figure 5-5). Those trends will be fetched from Twitter's **GET trends/place** API endpoint.

117

Figure 5-5. *The trends users can choose from to set as the "Selected Trend"*

From the screen shown in Figure 5-5, users can choose any one of the trends, and then the widget will display tweets related to that selected trend.

Doesn't that sound fun? Now let's take a look at the already existing code. We have already set up some basic stuff for you in TwitterTrends.

If you go to the **Project Navigator** and open the **TwitterTrends** project, you will see two main folders, that is, **TwitterTrends** and **TwitterTrendsWidget**. The **TwitterTrends** folder contains the files and folders related to the app, and the **TwitterTrendsWidget** folder contains the files and folders related to the widget. And there are certain files which are shared by both folders using **Target Membership**.

If you open the **TwitterTrends** folder in the **TwitterTrends** project, you will see the following folder structure:

```
TwitterTrends
├── Assets.xcassets
├── Extensions
│   └── View.swift
├── Info.plist
├── Models
│   ├── TrendTweets.swift
│   ├── Trends.swift
│   └── Tweets.swift
├── Preview\ Content
├── TwitterTrendsAPI.swift
├── TwitterTrendsApp.swift
├── ViewModel
│   └── TTViewModel.swift
└── Views
    ├── TrendsView.swift
    └── TweetsView.swift
```

In the **TwitterTrends** folder, other than **Assets.xcassets** and **Info.plist**, you will see the **Extensions** folder that contains a file named **View.swift**. It contains an extension of View that helps to handle the redacted(reason:) view modifier.

The **Models** folder contains **TrendTweets.swift**, **Trends.swift**, and **Tweets.swift**, which are the models used for decoding the response data received from Twitter's API. These files are used by both the app and the widget.

The **Preview Content** folder is a folder generated automatically by Xcode for storing the assets required for development purposes. Xcode does not include any assets in this folder in your release builds.

The next file is **TwitterTrendsAPI.swift**. It is responsible to handle communications with Twitter's API endpoints. This file is used by both the app and the widget to fetch tweets and trends from Twitter.

There is a file named **TwitterTrendsApp.swift** which is the entry point of the app.

Now, the only folders remaining are **ViewModel** and **Views**. The **ViewModel** folder consists of **TTViewModel.swift**, which contains the view model used by the app. And **Views** contains **TrendsView.swift** and **TweetsView.swift** which contain the user interface of the screens that display the top trends and the tweets related to those trends, respectively.

That's the description of the folders and files in the **TwitterTrends** folder.

There is another folder called **TwitterTrendsWidget** in the project. If you open it, you will see the folder structure given as follows:

```
TwitterTrendsWidget
├── Assets.xcassets
├── Info.plist
├── Model
│   └── TweetWidgetEntry.swift
├── Provider
│   └── TwitterProvider.swift
├── View
│   └── LargeWidgetView.swift
└── Widget
    └── TwitterTrendsWidget.swift
```

Currently, there are less files and folders in **TwitterTrendsWidget**. In addition to **Assets.xcassets** and **Info.plist**, there is a folder called **Model** that contains **TweetWidgetEntry.swift**. This file contains a TimelineEntry called TweetWidgetEntry which is vital for your widgets to work.

The **Provider** folder contains **TwitterProvider.swift**, which is the TimelineProvider of the widget.

Likewise, you can see another folder, **View**. It contains **LargeWidgetView.swift**, which contains the user interface of your widget.

Lastly, there is a folder called **Widget**, and it contains **TwitterTrendsWidget.swift**. It is the entry point of your widget.

Throughout this chapter, you will add more files and folders in your widget's folder and give your widget the power to fetch configuration options from a remote server.

Now, it's finally time to start working to give your widget the capability to communicate with Twitter's API to fetch the top trends and allow users to select any one of them to see the tweets related to that particular trend in the widget.

Time to Create a SiriKit Intent Definition File

This step is similar to that of the previous chapter. In this step, you will create an intent definition file, and using that file you will define configurable properties for your widgets. To create that file, follow the steps mentioned as follows:

1. Right-click the **TwitterTrendsWidget** folder in the project and click **New Group** to create a new folder. Name it **Intent**.

2. Now, right-click the **Intent** folder and click **New File...**.

3. In the dialog box that appears, select **SiriKit Intent Definition File**, name it **TwitterTrends. intentdefinition**, and create the file. While creating the file, make sure that both **TwitterTrendsWidgetExtension** and **TwitterTrends** targets are checked at the bottom of the dialog box.

4. Open **TwitterTrends.intentdefinition** and click the "+" icon at the bottom left of the intent file. After that, from the list of options, click **New Intent** (Figure 5-6).

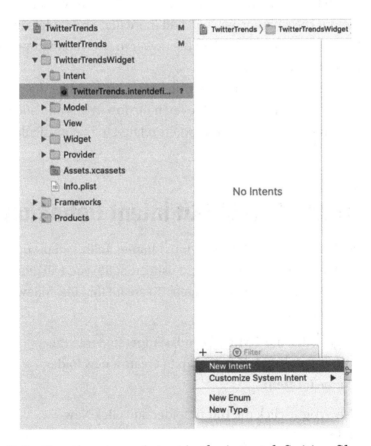

Figure 5-6. *Creating a new intent in the intent definition file*

5. Name the intent as **Trends** and modify some
    configuration of that intent. Since you are going to
    use the intent for widgets only, put a checkmark
    on **Intent is eligible for widgets** and remove
    checkmarks from **Intent is user-configurable in the
    Shortcuts app and Add to Siri** and **Intent is eligible
    for Siri Suggestions**.

6. Now, add a parameter named **selectedTrend** in
    the **Parameters** section by clicking the "+" button
    below it. Parameters are the properties that users
    will see and modify in the configuration screen of
    your widget to configure your widget. The display
    name that is displayed in the configuration screen
    of your widget (Figure 5-4) is automatically set to
    Selected Trend.

7. Then, change the type of the **selectedTrend**
    parameter to **Add Type...** (Figure 5-7).

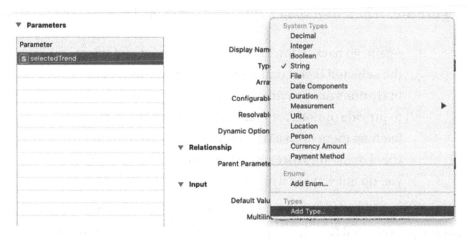

Figure 5-7. *Creating a parameter called "selectedTrend" and
changing its "Type" to "Add Type..."*

123

8. As soon as you click **Add Type...**, a new screen is displayed that appears similar to Figure 5-8. Change the name of the new type to **SelectedTrend** by typing it in the item under the **TYPES** header at the left.

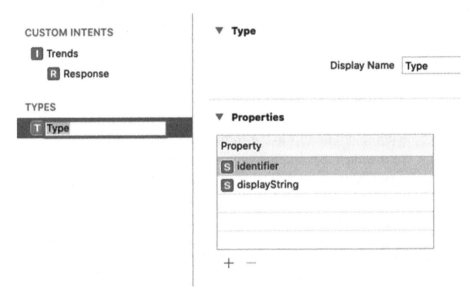

Figure 5-8. *The screen shown after clicking "Add Type."*

9. Again, go back to the **Trends** custom intent and select the **selectedTrend** parameter and add a checkmark in **Options are provided dynamically** as you want to provide options for that parameter dynamically by fetching them from a remote server. Also, remove the checkmark from **Siri can ask for value when run** since you do not want to work with Siri.

In this way, you have created an intent definition file and added the parameter, **selectedTrend**, using which users will select a trend of their choice from the widget's configuration screen.

Setting Up IntentHandler to Fetch Top Trends and Send Them to the Widget

Now, you have to add a mechanism to use **selectedTrend** parameter when the timeline is created. In the previous chapter, it was a straightforward and simple process, as you had an enum with a set of values you had defined or hard-coded. But this time, you are using a class, and things are going to be different.

So, first, you need to provide the widget the values that the **selectedTrend** parameter of **SelectedTrend** type can hold. For that, you will require an intent handler that will be responsible to fetch those values from the server and provide them to your widget.

1. In Xcode, go to **File ➤ New ➤ Target** to create a new target. In the dialog box that appears, select **Intents Extension** and click **Next**.

2. In the dialog box displayed, set **TwitterTrendsIntent** as **Product Name**, **Swift** as **Language**, and **None** as **Starting Point**. Make sure that **Include UI Extension** is not checked. And set **Project** to **TwitterTrends** and the value of **Embed in Application** to **TwitterTrends**. Then, click **Finish**. And click **Cancel** if you are asked to **Activate "TwitterTrendsIntent" scheme** because you will not have to activate that scheme to run your widget or app later.

   Now, a new folder called **TwitterTrendsIntent** is created in your project, and it contains **IntentHandler. swift** and **Info.plist**. The **IntentHandler.swift** file is where you will write the code to fetch the top trends from Twitter's server and send them to your widget.

125

3. Now, open the **TwitterTrends.intentdefinition** file
    in **TwitterTrendsWidget**'s **Intent** folder and update
    its **Target Membership** by adding a checkmark to
    TwitterTrendsIntent. Now, that file is accessible
    from **TwitterTrends**, **TwitterTrendsWidget**, and
    TwitterTrendsIntent.

4. One thing to keep in mind is that the
    TwitterTrendsIntent target should know the types of
    intents it can support. For that, select the **TwitterTrends**
    project (and not the TwitterTrends folder) located at the
    top of the **Project Navigator** to go to project settings.
    Now, select the **TwitterTrendsIntent** target under the
    TARGETS section and go to its **General** tab.

5. In the **General** tab of **TwitterTrendsIntent**, go to the
    Supported Intents section and click the "+" sign below
    it to add a new supported intent. Then the screen will
    look like Figure 5-9.

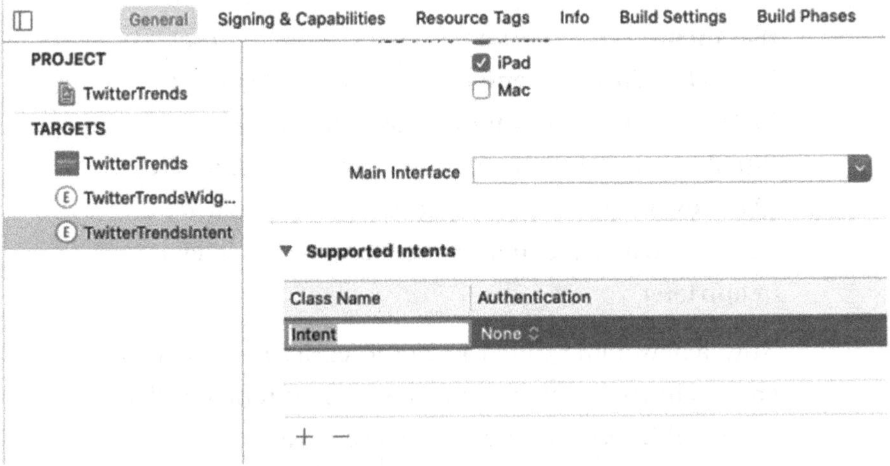

Figure 5-9. *The screen shown after clicking the "+" icon below*
Supported Intents

6.   Type **TrendsIntent** under the **Class Name**
heading. Since you have made **TwitterTrends.
intentdefinition** a member of the
TwitterTrendsIntent target in step 3, you will see a
suggestion as soon as you begin typing. The name
TrendsIntent has been generated automatically by
Xcode using the name of the custom intent, **Trends**,
you had added in **TwitterTrends.intentdefinition**
in step 5 of the **Time to Create a SiriKit Intent
Definition File** section of this chapter. At last, let
TrendsIntent's Authentication remain **None**.

7.   Now, open **IntentHandler.swift** in the
TwitterTrendsIntent folder. Right now, the
IntentHandler class is inheriting from the
INExtension class. Now make **IntentHandler**
conform to the **TrendsIntentHandling** protocol that
has been generated automatically by Xcode. After
doing that, your code in **IntentHandler.swift** will
look like Listing 5-1.

Listing 5-1. IntentHandler after conforming to
TrendsIntentHandling

```
import Intents

class IntentHandler: INExtension, TrendsIntentHandling {

    override func handler(for intent: INIntent) -> Any {
        return self
    }

}
```

8. As soon as you make `IntentHandler` conform to `TrendsIntentHandling`, Xcode will show you an error message saying, "Type 'IntentHandler' does not conform to protocol 'TrendsIntentHandling'. Do you want to add protocol stubs?" It is because you have not yet implemented the properties of the `TrendsIntentHandling` protocol in `IntentHandler`.

9. Click **Fix** to see Xcode generate the implementation of `provideSelectedTrendOptionsCollection(for:with:)`. This is where you will fetch top Twitter trends by communicating with its servers using `TwitterTrendsAPI`. But `TwitterTrendsAPI` is not currently accessible from **IntentHandler.swift**. So, you need to update its **Target Membership**.

10. Open **TwitterTrendsAPI.swift** in the **TwitterTrends** folder. Then, update its **Target Membership** by adding a checkmark to **TwitterTrendsIntent**. Now you will be able to access it from **IntentHandler. swift**.

11. Open **IntentHandler.swift** and implement `provide SelectedTrendOptionsCollection(for:with:)` by replacing the current implementation with the code given in Listing 5-2.

Listing 5-2. Implementation of provideSelectedTrendOptionsCollection(for:with:)

```
func provideSelectedTrendOptionsCollection(for intent:
TrendsIntent, with completion: @escaping (INObjectCollection
<SelectedTrend>?, Error?) -> Void) {
    // a
```

```
TwitterTrendsAPI.getAvailableTrends { response in
    // b
    switch response {
    // c
    case .success(let trends):
        // d
        if let firstTrend = trends.first {
            // e
            let availableTrends = firstTrend.trends
            // f
            let usableTrends: [SelectedTrend] =
            availableTrends.map { element in
                return SelectedTrend(identifier:
                element.query, display: element.name)
            }
            // g
            let inObjectCollection: INObjectCollection
            = INObjectCollection(items: usableTrends)
            completion(inObjectCollection, nil)
        }
    case .failure(let error):
        // h
        print(error.localizedDescription)
    }
}
}
```

After pasting the code of Listing 5-2, you must be
seeing a lot of errors. So, before describing what
is happening in Listing 5-2, first let's get rid of the
errors. If you go through the error messages, you will
see that Xcode is complaining about being unable
to find the types Trends, TrendTweets, Trend, and
Tweets. It is because TwitterTrendsAPI is now a

member of the **TwitterTrendsIntent** target also, but the structs that it uses (TrendTweets, Trend, and Tweets) are not the members of that target. So, you need to make those structs members of **TwitterTrendsIntent**.

From the **Models** folder of **TwitterTrends**, open **TrendTweets.swift** and update its **Target Membership** by putting a checkmark on **TwitterTrendsIntent**. Repeat the same for **Trends. swift** and **Tweets.swift** too.

12. Now build your project to find all the errors gone. Now, let's get back to knowing what is happening in Listing 5-2.

   a. Since the provideSelectedTrendOptions Collection(for:with:) method is the location from where you will fetch top Twitter trends and pass them as the options of the **selectedTrend** parameter, you begin the implementation by calling the getAvailableTrends(id:completion:) method of TwitterTrendsAPI.

   b. getAvailableTrends(id:completion:) returns response using its completion handler. response can either be .success or .failure. So, it is put through a switch case.

   c. If response has a .success value, it contains trends which is the data about the top trends.

   d. If you study the response format of Twitter's **GET trends/place** API endpoint, you will see that it returns an array with a single object. That single object is accessed using trends.first and stored in firstTrend.

e. Now, all the trends that have been fetched are stored in the `trends` property of `firstTrend`. So, they are accessed using `firstTrend.trends` and stored in `availableTrends`.

f. Since you have defined the data type of the **selectedTrend** parameter in **TwitterTrends. intentdefinition** as **SelectedTrend**, now you will have to convert the trends fetched from Twitter's API to that type. For that, `map` is run through all the values in the `availableTrends` array, and each iteration's `query` and `name` are used to create a new `SelectedTrend` instance. Then, they are stored in the `usableTrends` array, which is an array that stores `SelectedTrend` values.

g. In this step, `usableTrends` is passed into the `INObjectCollection` initializer and stored in `inObjectCollection`. Then, the completion handler is called by passing `inObjectCollection` as an argument. This is how the top trends fetched from Twitter's server are sent to the **selectedTrend** parameter of the widget.

h. In case `response` contains `.failure`, then its `error` property is accessed and printed into the console.

In this way, you fetched the trends from Twitter's API, converted them to the type of the **selectedTrend** parameter you created in **TwitterTrends.intentdefinition**, and passed them to **selectedTrend**.

Switching to IntentConfiguration

Right now, if you build and run your project, you will see that long pressing your widgets does not give the option to **Edit Widget**. It is because you have still not made necessary preparations to replace StaticConfiguration with IntentConfiguration. And to use IntentConfiguration, you will need a different timeline provider than the one you are using right now. Just follow the steps given to make "the big switch" to IntentConfiguration.

Create an IntentTimelineProvider

As mentioned previously, the first step to switch to IntentConfiguration is to set up an IntentTimelineProvider. Go through the given steps to set it up:

1. Right-click the **Provider** folder of the **TwitterTrendsWidget** folder, click **New File…**, and create a new Swift file named **TwitterTrendsIntentProvider.swift**. Make sure the **TwitterTrendsWidgetExtension** target is checked at the bottom of the dialog box before creating the file.

Note   You could use the existing **TwitterProvider.swift** file instead of creating **TwitterTrendsIntentProvider.swift**, but for better clarity, we recommend you to create **TwitterTrendsIntentProvider.swift**.

---

2. Open **TwitterTrendsIntentProvider.swift** and replace the existing code content with the code given in Listing 5-3.

Listing 5-3. Creating TwitterTrendsIntentProvider that conforms to IntentTimelineProvider

```
import SwiftUI
import WidgetKit

struct TwitterTrendsIntentProvider: IntentTimelineProvider {

}
```

3. In Listing 5-3, a struct named
    TwitterTrendsIntentProvider that conforms to
    IntentTimelineProvider is created. As soon as
    you add the code, Xcode will ask if you want to add
    protocol stubs. Click **Fix** and add them to see two
    typealiases, Entry and Intent, added to the struct.

4. In TwitterTrendsIntentProvider, replace the type
    placeholder of Entry with TweetWidgetEntry, a type
    of timeline entry. Also, replace the type placeholder
    of Intent with TrendsIntent, whose name was
    generated from the custom intent, Trends, you had
    created in **TwitterTrends.intentdefinition**.

Now your code should look like the code in Listing 5-4.

Listing 5-4. TwitterTrendsIntentProvider after adding Entry and Intent types

```
import SwiftUI
import WidgetKit

struct TwitterTrendsIntentProvider: IntentTimelineProvider {
    typealias Entry = TweetWidgetEntry
    typealias Intent = TrendsIntent
}
```

5. You will still see Xcode asking you to add protocol stubs. Add them too. Then, `placeholder(in:)`, `getSnapshot(for:in:completion:)`, and `getTimeline(for:in:completion:)` methods will get generated.

6. For implementing the `placeholder(in:)` and `getSnapshot(for:in:completion:)` methods of `TwitterTrendsIntentProvider`, you can copy the code from the `placeholder(in:)` and `getSnapshot(for:in:completion:)` methods of `TwitterProvider` in **TwitterProvider.swift** as the same implementations will work.

7. The `getTimeline(for:in:completion:)` method of `TwitterTrendsIntentProvider` is different than the `getTimeline(in:completion:)` method of `TwitterProvider` as `TwitterTrendsIntentProvider` conforms to `IntentTimelineProvider`, but `TwitterProvider` conforms to `TimelineProvider`. And the `getTimeline(for:in:completion:)` method of `TwitterTrendsIntentProvider` allows you to access the data from the configuration of the widget.

    In the current scenario, you will access the selected trend from the widget's configuration and use it to perform the API call to fetch tweets related to that selected trend. In case there isn't a selected trend, you will make the widget fetch the tweets related to the first trend in the array of the trends fetched from Twitter's API. And you will do everything in `getTimeline(for:in:completion:)`.

Before you start working on getTimeline(for:in:
completion:), let's first create a method, create
TimelineFromTweets(response:), to create a
timeline from the tweets that will be fetched from
the API. Then, you can call this method from
getTimeline(for:in:completion:). This will
make the code readable and easy to understand.
Copy the code given in Listing 5-5 and paste it in
TwitterTrendsIntentProvider.

Listing 5-5. Creating the createTimelineFromTweets(response:)
method

```
func createTimelineFromTweets(response: Result<TrendTweets,
Error>) -> Timeline<TweetWidgetEntry> {
      // a
      let currentDate = Date()
      // b
      let refreshDate = Calendar.current.date(byAdding:
      .minute, value: 30, to: currentDate)!
      // c
      var entry = TweetWidgetEntry(date: refreshDate,
      statuses: Tweets.dummyTweets, trendTitle: "")
      // d
      var timeline = Timeline(entries: [entry], policy:
      .after(refreshDate))

      // e
      switch response {
      case let .success(tweets):
          // f
          entry = TweetWidgetEntry(date: refreshDate,
          statuses: tweets.statuses, trendTitle: tweets.title)
```

```
            timeline = Timeline(entries: [entry], policy:
            .after(refreshDate))
            return timeline
        case let .failure(error):
            // g
            print(error.localizedDescription)
            return timeline
        }
    }
```

In Listing 5-5, you created a method createTimeline
FromTweets(response:) that has response as the
parameter and returns a timeline. In it, the following
things have been done:

a. At the beginning, the current date is stored in
    currentDate.

b. Now, the date after adding 30 minutes to
    currentDate is generated and stored in
    refreshDate. You will use it later to set up the
    widget's refresh policy.

c. In this step, the TweetWidgetEntry timeline
    entry is created by passing refreshDate, dummy
    tweets, and an empty title string to its initializer.
    Then, it is stored in entry.

d. Now a timeline is created using entry and by
    setting the refresh policy to make the widget
    request a new timeline after 30 minutes. In this
    way, the timeline is created.

e. As response may either have a .success value
    or a .failure value, it is put through a switch
    case. If response has a .success value, it uses

tweets received with .success and creates a new TweetWidgetEntry by using tweets' title and statuses properties. Then, the value of the entry variable is replaced by this new entry. And the value of the timeline variable is also replaced with a new timeline created using the new value of entry, and therefore the timeline is returned.

f.   In case response contains .failure, the error variable is accessed, and its value is printed into the console. Also, since the method must return a timeline, the timeline variable with dummy tweets and empty title (that you created in steps "c" and "d") is returned.

8.   Now it's time to start working in the getTimeline (for:in:completion:) method. Replace the existing getTimeline(for:in:completion:) method with the code given in Listing 5-6.

Listing 5-6. Implementation of the getTimeline(for:in:completion:) method

```
func getTimeline(for configuration: TrendsIntent, in context:
Context, completion: @escaping (Timeline<TweetWidgetEntry>) ->
Void) {
        // a
        if let trend = configuration.selectedTrend {
            let selectedTrend = Trend(name: trend.
            displayString, query: trend.identifier!)
            TwitterTrendsAPI.getTweets(on: selectedTrend) {
            response in
```

```
            completion(createTimelineFromTweets(response:
            response))
        }
    } else { // b
        TwitterTrendsAPI.getLatestTweets { response in
            completion(createTimelineFromTweets(response:
            response))
        }
    }
}
```

In Listing 5-6, the implementation of the getTime
line(for:in:completion) method is given. The
following things take place in Listing 5-6:

a.   This method checks for two cases – the
      first is the case when there exists a value of
      selectedTrend in configuration, and the
      second one is the case when selectedTrend
      does not contain any value. The selectedTrend
      property is the parameter that you had created
      in **TwitterTrends.intentdefinition** in the
      previous sections of this chapter.

      In the current step, the code checks if users have
      already selected a trend from their configuration
      screen. Thus, if users have selected a trend, meaning
      that there exists a value in selectedTrend, it is stored
      in trend, and a new instance of Trend is created by
      using the trend's displayString and identifier.

      Then, the getTweets(on:completion:) method
      of TwitterTrendsAPI is called to fetch the tweets
      related to that trend. When a response is received,

the completion handler of the getTimeline(for:in:
completion:) method is called by passing the call
to createTimelineFromTweets(response:) as its
argument.

The createTimelineFromTweets(response:)
takes the response received from the API call as
an argument, generates a timeline, and returns it.
At last, the completion handler of getTimeline(for:
in:completion:) uses that timeline, and a timeline is
created for the widget.

b.   But in case users have not selected any trend
(or there is no value in the selectedTrend
property of configuration), the
getLatestTweets(completion:) method of
TwitterTrendsAPI is called. This method first
fetches all the trends from Twitter's API, selects
the first trend from the API's response, fetches
the tweets related to that trend, and returns it
as response. On receiving the response, the
completion handler of the getTimeline(for:
in:completion:) method is called by passing
the call to createTimelineFromTweets
(response:) as its argument.

Then, the createTimelineFromTweets(response:)
uses the response received from the API call as an
argument, generates a timeline, and returns it.
At last, the completion handler of getTimeline(for:
in:completion:) uses that timeline, and a timeline
is created for the widget.

In this way, you created an `IntentTimelineProvider`, which is necessary for switching to `IntentConfiguration`.

Make the Switch to IntentConfiguration

Now you are all set to make the switch to `IntentConfiguration`. If you open the **TwitterTrendsWidget.swift** file of the **Widget** folder in the **TwitterTrendsWidget** folder, you will see that `StaticConfiguration` has been used right now in the body of `TwitterTrendsWidget`.

In `TwitterTrendsWidget`, create a variable, `dynamicConfiguration`, by using the code given in Listing 5-7.

Listing 5-7. Creation of a dynamicConfiguration variable

```
var dynamicConfiguration: some WidgetConfiguration {
        IntentConfiguration(kind: kind, intent: TrendsIntent.
        self, provider: TwitterTrendsIntentProvider()) { entry in
            LargeWidgetView(tweets: entry.statuses, title:
            entry.trendTitle)
        }
        .supportedFamilies([.systemLarge])
        .configurationDisplayName("Tweets")
        .description("Tweets Trending Today")
    }
```

In Listing 5-7, a variable named `dynamicConfiguration` is created which returns an `IntentConfiguration` initializer. It uses the value of `TwitterTrendsWidget`'s kind variable, `TrendsIntent` as its intent, and the initializer of `TwitterTrendsIntentProvider` as its timeline provider. All the other lines of code are similar to that of the `StaticConfiguration` that exists in the body of `TwitterTrendsWidget`.

Now, replace the body of `TwitterTrendsWidget` with the code given in Listing 5-8.

Listing 5-8. Using dynamicConfiguration in the body of
TwitterTrendsWidget

```
var body: some WidgetConfiguration {
        dynamicConfiguration
    }
```

The code given in Listing 5-8 replaces the StaticConfiguration with
the dynamicConfiguration variable that contains IntentConfiguration.

Well done! You have switched to IntentConfiguration.

Test – Test – Test!

Uninstall all the existing installations of **TwitterTrends** in your device or
simulator. Now, select the **TwitterTrends** scheme and run it. To test your
widget, add the TwitterTrends widget to your homescreen and try editing
it. You should see a configuration screen similar to the one shown in
Figure 5-4. Tap on **Choose** to see a screen where you can see a list of trends
fetched from Twitter. This screen will look similar to Figure 5-5. From that
screen, select any trend and go back to your homescreen. Now, in your
widget, you should see the tweets related to that particular trend you had
selected.

Awesome job! We hope you had fun.

Summary

Congratulations on making it this far! In this chapter, you learned how
you can make your widget fetch data from a server so that you can use
those data as configuration options for the parameter in your configurable
widget. Some part of this chapter must have been like a revision of the

previous chapters to you. And we hope you enjoyed following along and learning. If you have any confusions, please check out the final version of the code by opening the final project folder named **TwitterTrendsFinal** in **TwitterTrends.zip**.

Now you are able to create any kind of widgets – be it a widget that can or cannot be configured or a widget whose parameter has hard-coded configuration options or dynamic configuration options fetched from a server. You have mastered them all.

We wish you luck for the future. Happy coding!

Index